Glorious Redemptive Act of the Sanctuary of God

by
Daniel LeFebo

TEACH Services, Inc.
PUBLISHING
www.TEACHServices.com

Copyright © 2012 TEACH Services, Inc.
ISBN-13: 978-1-57258-695-6 (Paperback)
ISBN-13: 978-1-57258-696-3 (Hardback)
ISBN-13: 978-1-57258-697-0 (Epub)
ISBN-13: 978-1-57258-701-4 (Kindle)
Library of Congress Control Number: 2011941908

All scripture quotations, unless otherwise indicated, are taken from the King James Version Bible.

Published by

TEACH Services, Inc.

P U B L I S H I N G

www.TEACHServices.com

Table of Contents

Acknowledgement

First and foremost I dedicate this book to God. I praise Him for helping me to understand the mystery of the sanctuary of God and giving me the inspiration to write down the words in this book. God is more than amazing. I utter His everlasting greatness and His impartial love to all creation now and forevermore. His love and care for me is immeasurable and unlimited in the midst of stormy gales and fiery furnaces. My eyes have seen it. My continual praises go to God and Him alone.

I want to thank Mr. and Mrs. Lee Davis who sent me to the seminary at Andrews University in Berrien Springs, Michigan. I will forever treasure their financial support, prayers, and nurturing spirit more than anybody ever could know. May the God of heaven bless you, Mom and Dad, as you have blessed me.

I want to thank my friend Mike Stumvoll who made this book possible by paying for its publication. Mike's love for the Savior is manifested by his support of promoting the word of the truth in all means possible. Mike always finds creative ways to reach families for Christ using the talents God has given him.

I want to thank Christeen Williams who has always encouraged me through her prayers, finances, and guidance, including recommending me to TEACH Services, Inc.

I also thank Joyce Matthews who typed the manuscript of this book in the midst of her very busy schedule.

I want to thank Kalie Kelch who edited the manuscript and prepared it for publication. Kalie, you are greatly appreciated for your graciousness and professionalism.

I also want to thank God for the writings of Ellen G. White and Pastor Jack Sequera. Their books helped me to see the sanctuary ministry in our era in two different ways for the same purpose, besides the patriarchs, prophets, and apostles.

Last but not least, I thank my dear wife Be-emnet M. Meshesha and my five-and-a-half-year-old son, Emmanuel G. LeFebo, for their patience, love, and support. They have stuck by me throughout the process of me writing this book.

Preface

On July 9, 2010, around 10 a.m., while I was sitting in my dining room, I felt a strong impression from God to write about the sanctuary. I froze in fear as I said to God, "It is too complex." But God impressed upon my heart that He would simplify it for me to the point that everyone could understand the mystery of the sanctuary ministry.

I then remembered my personal commitment with God to only write material that would glorify Him. Again, I felt God speak to my heart, instructing me to write about His sanctuary. I burst out in tears and sat paralyzed in my chair at the dining room table, shaking as I thought about the task ahead of me.

I didn't know where to start. But the Spirit of God guided me to start at Creation. The sanctuary of God is the very presence of God, not just the space or geographic location. God truly was with humanity even from the beginning of time. When God created man, God shared his own personal life with him. God created man in His own image and likeness and then breathed life into him (Gen. 1:26, 27; 2:7). God shared His own life with humanity. Sharing Himself with Adam and Eve was the establishment of a relationship with humankind. Unfortunately, the relationship was interrupted by sin.

After sin entered the world, God set in motion a plan to redeem humanity from the wages of sin and re-establish a relationship with His people. It was fulfilled on the cross when God gave His only Son for the ransom of sin (John 3:16, 17).

Sanctuary means the house of God. In other words, it is the indwelling or habitation of God. Humanity was created to be the indwelling place or habitation of God. The physical actuality of the sanctuary ministry was revealed during Moses' leadership in the wilderness when the children of Israel left Egypt and the house of bondage and freely worshipped God in the sanctuary, the house of God. The children of Israel were no longer slaves, and they were free to worship the only true and eternal God.

When God gave Moses instructions to build the sanctuary, He told him to build it among the people so that God could dwell in their midst and protect, teach, reprove, correct, and instruct them in righteousness (2 Tim. 3:16). Moses was assigned to construct or structure the tent in the pattern of the heavenly sanctuary, which was not built by man but by God's own hand. God gave Moses the pattern of heaven on earth when He instructed him to build the sanctuary so that He could dwell in the midst of His people.

On that Friday morning in July as I sat in my dining room, I committed to writing about the sanctuary. As I felt impressed by God, I committed to exploring the subject from Creation to redemption and writing in a way as to eliminate fear, confusion, misunderstandings, and false doctrines.

As human beings, we often make our own religion or belief system if we do not fully understand a subject in an effort to feel secure. The only way for humanity to understand God's messages for us today is through diligent study of His Word. As we seek to understand the meaning of the sanctuary and the atonement of God, the cross of Christ was, is, and will be the most important point to study as it is the highest meaning of the sanctuary ministry.

This book sheds light on the meaning and purpose of the sanctuary and how humanity needs the immediate presence of God's indwelling within us every day, both on this old world and in the new world to come. Today's sanctuary is God's own personal presence with His people on earth; humankind is the temple of God (1 Cor. 3:16, 17; 6:19, 20; 2 Cor. 6:16). And in heaven and the new earth God Himself will be the temple (Rev. 21:3, 22).

Introduction

"For I am not ashamed of the gospel of Christ: for it is the power of God unto salvation to every one that believeth; to the Jew first, and also to the Greek. For therein is the righteousness of God revealed from faith to faith: as it is written, the just shall live by faith. For the wrath of God is revealed from heaven against all ungodliness and unrighteousness of men, who hold the truth in unrighteousness; because that which may be known of God is manifest in them; for God hath shewed it unto them. For the invisible things of him from the creation of the world are clearly seen, being understood by the things that are made, even his eternal power and Godhead; so that they are without excuse" (Rom. 1:16-20).

The gospel of the sanctuary is God's personal presence from creation with Adam and Eve and with all humanity throughout the ages. When the human race fell into sin, God renewed His covenant relationship with Adam and Eve by killing an innocent animal and covering the nakedness of Adam and Eve with sheep's skin, which was an indicator of God's mercy upon Adam and Eve and their descendants and all creation. Unfortunately, Adam's descendents grew wicked. God cleansed wickedness from the earth and renewed a new covenant relationship with the patriarchs—Noah, Abraham, Joseph, and Moses—the prophets—Isaiah, Jesus, and the apostles—and with those of us who are waiting for the second advent of Christ.

Unfortunately, after re-establishing a relationship with His people, it was only a matter of time before they ran back to serve the enemy. Throughout the Bible, God was disgraced and disrespected at the hands of His people. But

God, who is love and merciful, never gave up. God never changed His nature and character. God is omniscient, omnipotent, and omnipresent.

God's original plan for humanity was unadulterated commune with Him. This is the truth that is revealed in the message of the sanctuary of God, which is the central theme of this book. As we begin, we will be looking at where the problem lies and what the alternative solution for the problem is.

Chapter 1

The Patriarchs and the Sanctuary

The problem is a lack of understanding of the sanctuary ministry of God in the life of Adam and Eve, Noah's children, Abraham's children, Moses, and throughout the ages. The problem also lies in the lack of understanding in regards to the modern sanctuary ministry in the Christian's life and the sanctuary ministry in the heavenly place before and after the millennium. These cause the greatest misunderstandings of the true gospel of Christ Jesus, the redemptive act of God, the confusion or fornication of mixing true and false ideas, and the fall of the truthfulness of Christianity.

The first thing that Lucifer, the fallen angel, did was to infect humanity with his own character, which is known by us today as the mystery of iniquity. This is the mystery of wickedness or ungodliness.

The mystery of iniquity is sin, wickedness, ungodliness, transgression, and rebellion—all character traits of Satan. God didn't create iniquity in Satan. Satan developed this character while he was at and in the very presence of God in heaven, serving God as the angel Lucifer.

Satan proved to be the murderer of God in an attempt to overthrow the throne of God. Isaiah, Ezekiel, and John the Revelator explicitly described this event:

> "Son of man, take up a lamentation upon the king of Tyrus, and say unto him, Thus saith the Lord GOD; Thou sealest up the sum, full of wisdom, and perfect in beauty. Thou hast been in Eden the garden of God; every precious stone was thy covering, the sardius, topaz, and the diamond, the beryl, the onyx, and the jasper, the sapphire, the emerald, and the carbuncle, and gold: the workmanship of thy tabrets

and of thy pipes was prepared in thee in the day that thou wast created. Thou art the anointed cherub that covereth; and I have set thee so: thou wast upon the holy mountain of God; thou hast walked up and down in the midst of the stones of fire. Thou wast perfect in thy ways from the day that thou wast created, till iniquity was found in thee" (Ezek. 28:12-15).

"How art thou fallen from heaven, O Lucifer, son of the morning! how art thou cut down to the ground, which didst weaken the nations! For thou hast said in thine heart, I will ascend into heaven, I will exalt my throne above the stars of God: I will sit also upon the mount of the congregation, in the sides of the north: I will ascend above the heights of the clouds; I will be like the most High" (Isa. 14:12-14).

"And there was war in heaven: Michael and his angels fought against the dragon; and the dragon fought and his angels, and prevailed not; neither was their place found any more in heaven. And the great dragon was cast out, that old serpent, called the Devil, and Satan, which deceiveth the whole world: he was cast out into the earth, and his angels were cast out with him.... Therefore rejoice, ye heavens, and ye that dwell in them. Woe to the inhabiters of the earth and of the sea! for the devil is come down unto you, having great wrath, because he knoweth that he hath but a short time" (Rev. 12:7-12).

When Satan came to this earth, he developed his plan by aborting the everlasting sanctuary of God, which was the human person, which God had created in His own image and likeness and the only creation with which He had shared the divine breath of life, that humankind and God could dwell together forever. In Genesis 1:26, 27 and 2:7 Satan deceived Adam and Eve and caused the fall of humanity.

"Now the serpent was more subtil than any beast of the field which the LORD God had made. And he said unto the woman, Yea, hath God said, Ye shall not eat of every tree of the garden? And the woman said unto the serpent, We may eat of the fruit of the trees of the garden: But of the fruit of the tree which is in the midst of the garden, God hath said, Ye shall not eat of it, neither shall ye touch it, lest ye die. And the serpent said unto the woman, Ye shall not surely die: For God doth know that in the day ye eat thereof, then your eyes shall be opened, and ye shall be as gods, knowing good and evil.

"And when the woman saw that the tree was good for food, and that it was pleasant to the eyes, and a tree to be desired to make one wise, she took of the fruit thereof, and did eat, and gave also unto her husband with her; and he did eat. And the eyes of them both were opened, and they knew that they were naked; and they sewed fig leaves together, and made themselves aprons. And they heard the voice of the LORD God walking in the garden in the cool of the day: and Adam and his wife hid themselves from the presence of the LORD God amongst the trees of the garden. And the LORD God called unto Adam, and said unto him, Where art thou? And he said, I heard thy voice in the garden, and I was afraid, because I was naked; and I hid myself" (Gen. 3:1-10).

Now, Satan was not only successful in separating himself from such an Omniscient, Omnipresent, and Omnipotent God but he also played in the devastating role of separating humanity from God. Humankind was created to be a sanctuary of God, where humankind was to be the co-ruler of the earth.

"And God said, Let us make man in our image, after our likeness: and let them have dominion over the fish of the sea, and over the fowl of the air, and over the cattle, and over all the earth, and over every creeping thing that creepeth upon the earth" (Gen. 1:26).

Satan deceived Adam and Eve and caused them to disobey God. Thus, Adam and Eve became the slaves of Satan, sin, self, and death. Humankind was locked into these rules of tyranny under the dominion of Satan.

Satan not only aborted the original plan of God for humankind but in the process he also fully developed his character of sin and iniquity. Satan discovered the most fertile ground to establish the power of sin by capturing the human mind.

Satan deceitfully and forcefully began to control human beings. Satan could not mature to his own full character in heaven. In Isaiah 14:12-14 we clearly see how Satan wanted to overthrow the throne of God and control the universe and be like the Most High. Unfortunately, that strategy failed. Satan then decided to use another method to accomplish his wickedness—he deceived a third of the angels in heaven and humankind on earth, too. Satan caused an interruption in the perfect plan of God. God's plan was love and total harmony between God and creation and between creation and creation. All was to be in harmony (unity) and undisrupted love.

God was unable to dwell with Adam and Eve because they ran away from Him when God came to fellowship with them during the cool hour of the day. Again, Adam and Eve hid themselves from God. This became the pattern of all people to run away from God.

Then God came and covered the nakedness of Adam and Eve with animal skins because they would last longer and be better for them than the fig leaves which would not last them more than a few hours in the dry hot sun. The leaves would have dried up quickly. The fig leaf was a symbol of self-righteousness, while the skins were a symbol of the righteousness of God, which is the everlasting lovingkindness of God.

Human righteousness fades away because it is corrupted with selfishness, but the righteousness of God cannot be corrupted with selfishness. It doesn't depend on a changeable condition. I will discuss this in more detail later on in the book.

Even after all of this, God still wanted to establish a relationship with the sons of Adam, Cain and Abel. Unfortunately, selfishness and disobedience reared its ugly head, and Cain killed Abel and then ran away from God (Gen. 4). After that, the sons of God married the daughters of men, causing God to regret creating humankind (Gen. 6:1-3).

Because human beings went farther and farther away from God, He decided to eradicate sin and sinners from the earth with a giant flood (Gen. 7:1; 8:22).

God made another covenant of abiding with Noah and his children's generations:

"And God said, This is the token of the covenant which I make between me and you and every living creature that is with you, for perpetual generations: I do set my bow in the cloud, and it shall be for a token of a covenant between me and the earth. And it shall come to pass, when I bring a cloud over the earth, that the bow shall be seen in the cloud: And I will remember my covenant, which is between me and you and every living creature of all flesh; and the waters shall no more become a flood to destroy all flesh. And the bow shall be in the cloud; and I will look upon it, that I may remember the everlasting covenant between God and every living creature of all flesh that is upon the earth. And God said unto Noah, This is the token of the covenant, which I have established between me and all flesh that is upon the earth" (Gen. 9:12-17).

Unfortunately, Noah's descendents also ran away from God, even to the point that they began to build their own tower of escape.

"And the whole earth was of one language, and of one speech. And it came to pass, as they journeyed from the east, that they found a plain in the land of Shinar; and they dwelt there. And they said one to another, Go to, let us make brick, and burn them thoroughly. And they had brick for stone, and slime had they for morter. And they said, Go to, let us build us a city and a tower, whose top may reach unto heaven; and let us make us a name, lest we be scattered abroad upon the face of the whole earth.

"And the LORD came down to see the city and the tower, which the children of men builded. And the LORD said, Behold, the people is one, and they have all one language; and this they begin to do: and now nothing will be restrained from them, which they have imagined to do. Go to, let us go down, and there confound their language, that they may not understand one another's speech. So the LORD scattered them abroad from thence upon the face of all the earth: and they left off to build the city. Therefore is the name of it called Babel; because the LORD did there confound the language of all the earth: and from thence did the LORD scatter them abroad upon the face of all the earth" (Gen. 11:1-9).

God later came to Abraham and started a new relationship with him and his descendents. With Abraham, God shared His thoughts, guided him as a personal friend, and shared a meal at Abraham's home (Gen. 12 and 18). God enjoyed an intimate relationship with Abraham, even showing him the sacrificial system by asking Abraham to offer up Isaac, the son of promise, as a sacrifice (Gen. 22:1-18). This was a foretelling of how God was going to give up His only Son, Jesus Christ, for the world (John 3:16-18).

So God developed a personal and familial relationship with Abraham. It didn't take long for the children of Jacob, who were the great-grandsons of Abraham, to sell Joseph the dreamer, God's messenger. But years later they were left desolate under the curse of famine and draught while the land of the unbelievers prospered because of the "dreamer" who had been sold to a foreign land, which they would eventually visit to buy food.

Whenever people run away from God or ban Him from their lives, they are left desolate and miserable. Thus was the case with Jacob's descendents who were sold into 400 years of miserable slavery.

Again, after the exodus, God reinstituted a new covenant with His people through the Ten Commandments and the strong bind of the sanctuary ministry with Moses and the children of Israel (Exod. 20:1-17; 25:8, 9; 29:42-46).

This is God's final covenant relationship with His people—the Ten Commandments and sanctuary ministry. This is the everlasting gospel of God for humankind and the ever-binding relationship of God with the whole human race. That is the only reason it is called the atonement day ministry. This ministry is the only one-way covenant.

God invites us to participate in it. He knew that the children of Israel were bankrupt and corrupt and that they couldn't make this glorious atonement with Him. So God, with His great mercy and kindness, called the children of Israel, with all of their complaints and murmurings, to obey the Ten Commandments and follow the sanctuary services in an effort to bind their relationship.

God, by His own Word, said, "I will dwell in the midst of [my people]" (Ezek. 43:7). And He built a sanctuary among the people. The sanctuary is God's presence, not a geographic location. The sanctuary is important, not because it was built in the wilderness, but because God's immediate presence or atonement was above all expression of glory and majesty of the sanctuary. The glory and majesty was not to or for a wooden temple, but it was the good news for human beings and the glory to God that His people could worship Him in spirit and in truth. The greatest pitfall was when the children of Israel focused on the wooden sanctuary and location on the earth, instead of their relationship with God. The nation of Israel is the only God-favored nation on earth, which is still creating many problems, even today.

Definitely, Israel was elected to be the messenger for the entire human race just as Adam was the father to the entire human race. Noah, Abraham, and Moses were the fathers of the new generations—all these men received direct covenant calls or interactions with God to begin a new generation of followers. But in all instances, the descendents of these patriarchs fell away from God.

The children of Noah began to build the Tower of Babel, offering a false sense of protection. So God scattered them to all of the faces of the earth. Then God called Abraham from among the confused nation of the children of Noah and established a new covenant with him and his children. Abraham's descendants failed miserably and fell into slavery in Egypt.

Next, God called Moses and delivered the children of Israel and re-established a new covenant to be among them continually, but the children of Israel once again turned away soon after they came out of Egypt. They committed an even worse sin in the sight of God than the nations who did not have a true experience with God because they knew God.

Because of the unfailing love of God, the sanctuary ministry continued via the prophets. God directly sent messages through the prophets word by word, guiding them in what to do. Whenever the nation began to stray away from God and the prophets would cry for help, God would answer the elected nation of Israel, which was His own seed to save the world.

The biblical background of the sanctuary started in the Garden of Eden where God and Adam and Eve were together. Due to the interruption of sin, the physical contact or unity that God had directly with humanity was broken for a long time. God Himself re-established a new covenant relationship through the sanctuary ministry via Moses in the wilderness and the construction of the physical sanctuary that God could dwell in among the people (Exod. 25:8, 9; 29:42-46).

When the children of Israel left Egypt, God sought to reside with His people in a visible way through the sanctuary of the wilderness. God designed the pattern of the earthly sanctuary after the heavenly sanctuary. The holy place and Most Holy Place were for the remission of sins. The daily sacrifice with the priests, along with the annual sacrifice that the High Priest offered, was a portrayal of Christ in heaven.

If Christians understand the entire design, structure, and purpose of the sanctuary, then they would understand that it is the hope of glory for all Christians. If the wilderness sanctuary in Bible times, the modern sanctuary here on earth, and the heavenly sanctuary are not clearly understood, then Christians are in the dark.

The whole gospel of Jesus Christ is based on the sanctuary and the sanctuary ministry from the beginning to the end. The entire gospel is Christ and Christ alone. Everything about the sanctuary points to Christ and His righteousness. The sanctuary is the covenant relationship of God with humankind. The covenant relationship is God's "at-one-ment" with His people.

His atonement is His reconciliation with humanity. The reconciliation of God was manifested through the life giving love of His only Son on the cross for the redemption of the human race at the cost of His own Son's life (John 3:16-18).

God eventually united humanity forever and ever. "That they all may be one; as thou, Father, art in me, and I in thee, that they also may be one in us: that the world may believe that thou hast sent me. And the glory which thou gavest me I have given them; that they may be one, even as we are one: I in them, and thou in me, that they may be made perfect in one; and that the world may know that thou hast sent me, and hast loved them, as thou hast loved me" (John 17:21-23).

God presented in the wilderness courtyard the representation of Jesus, the holy place as a type of the Holy Spirit, and the Most Holy Place as a type of the Father in heaven. This is why the earthly sanctuary was called the pattern of heaven. The representation of the sanctuary is an amazingly glorious message for Christians.

As we've learned thus far, the sanctuary is the dwelling of God in our midst. God established his sanctuary among His people at multiple times throughout the Old Testament, re-establishing his covenant with the patriarchs and their descendents and instructing them in the ways of the kingdom of God.

Chapter 2

The Gospel of the Sanctuary

When the apostle Paul said, "I am not ashamed of the gospel of Christ," he was saying that he was not ashamed of Christ because Christ is the power of all creation. Paul understood that Christ is the good news for the salvation of all creation (Rom. 1:16; 8:21-25).

Actually, the sanctuary ministry is not only a personal covenant relationship but also the saving act of God from its beginning. The Day of Atonement in the sanctuary was the saving act of God. The various sections of the sanctuary such as the courtyard, holy place, and Most Holy Place, also known as Holy of Holies, point to the ultimate sacrificial service of Christ Jesus. In later days in the New Testament era, the sanctuary points to the ministry of the eternal saving act of God for all humankind (John 3:16-18).

The sanctuary is defined in the biblical view as God's reaching out to reconcile Himself with the weak and sinful and loving the human race who hates Him (Rom. 5:6-10; 2 Cor. 5:18-20), but God reached out to make humankind a part of His household. God not only made peace with humanity but He made us believers in Him, kings and priests (Rev. 1:5, 6), heirs (Rom. 8:17), branches (John 15:4, 5), the apple of His eye (Zech. 2:8), and ambassadors for His kingdom (2 Cor. 5:20; Eph. 6:20). We also know that God engraved us upon the palm of His hands (Isa. 49:16). It is evident that God loves us with an everlasting love.

This act of reconciliation and redemption of God is what the Bible calls atonement or "at-one-ment" if you separate the word. The sanctuary ministry or sanctuary service is the ministry of "God with us," as is shown in the Old (Exod. 25:8, 22) and New Testaments (Matt. 1:18; 23:20; Gal. 2:20; 4:4;

Heb. 1:5, 6). The miraculous incarnation itself is the sanctuary ("at-one-ment") of God. The word sanctuary represents God's dwelling place. Emmanuel is God with us or in the midst of us. The whole purpose of the sanctuary is for God to spend time with His people.

But who are His people? His people are the weak, lost, and helpless sinners who seek deliverance from Satan's slavery and turn to God for deliverance. God, through the incarnation, manifested His divinity or glory to the visible human form. The merciful God graciously revealed Himself to humanity and dwelled with humanity.

"In the beginning was the Word, and the Word was with God, and the Word was God. The same was in the beginning with God. All things were made by him; and without him was not any thing made.... And the Word was made flesh, and dwelt among us, (and we beheld his glory, the glory as of the only begotten of the Father,) full of grace and truth" (John 1:1-3, 14). The incarnation was predicted throughout the sanctuary ministries spoken by God and performed by the patriarchs and prophets, through the high priests as the type pointing to the antitype of fulfillment of the incarnation, crucifixion, burial, resurrection, ascension, and second advent of Christ.

One of the greatest messengers of God for the last days stated, "The all-merciful God shrouded His glory in a most humble type, that Moses could look upon it and live. So in the pillar of cloud by day and the pillar of fire by night, God communicated with Israel, revealing to men His will, and imparting to them His grace. God's glory was subdued, and His majesty veiled, that the weak vision of finite men might behold it. So Christ was to come in 'the body of our humiliation' (Philippians 3:21, R.V.), "in the likeness of men.".…

"God commanded Moses for Israel, 'Let them make Me a sanctuary; that I may dwell among them' (Exodus 25:8), and He abode in the Sanctuary, in the midst of His people. Through all their weary wandering in the desert, the symbol of His presence was with them. So Christ set up His tabernacle in the midst of our human encampment. He pitched His tent by the side of the tents of men, that He might dwell among us and make us familiar with His divine character and life.…

"Since Jesus came to dwell with us, we now know that God is acquainted with our trials, and sympathizes with our griefs. Every son and daughter of

Adam may understand that our Creator is the friend of sinners. For in every doctrine of grace, every promise of joy, every deed of love, every divine attraction presented in the Savior's life on earth, we see 'God with us'" (Ellen G. White, *The Desire of Ages*, pp. 23, 24).

The gospel of the sanctuary is the revelation of the grace of God. The grace of God is the manifestation of God's personal love gift to the undeserving person or enemy. All of this God performs in the ministry of the sanctuary; therefore, the sanctuary is the activity of God in the midst of a people who don't deserve it, but who He has loved since the beginning of time. This is His act of personal righteousness from Himself for us.

This revelation of the true grace of God or righteousness of God is His personal infinite wisdom for finite man who is His enemy, sold into sin. Therefore, the grace of God or the free gift of God is given to us, weakened sinners (Rom. 5:6, 8, 10), in complete love.

God's free gift of love is clearly revealed in the wisdom of the gospel message that Paul wrote to the Philippians: "Let this mind be in you, which was also in Christ Jesus: Who, being in the form of God, thought it not robbery to be equal with God: But made himself of no reputation, and took upon him the form of a servant, and was made in the likeness of men: And being found in fashion as a man, he humbled himself, and became obedient unto death, even the death of the cross" (Phil. 2:5-8).

The emptying or giving of self is true righteousness that can only come from the Creator of man and nature. This personal, loving covenant relationship is a service of the grace of God. This is His own righteousness or His only loving grace to those who are unlovable or unacceptable. Jeremiah said, "In his days Judah shall be saved, and Israel shall dwell safely; and this is his name whereby he shall be called, THE LORD OUR RIGHTEOUSNESS" (Jer. 23:6). God Himself is righteousness. He is righteousness from His sanctuary, from His throne, from His actions (ministries in heaven and on earth), and from His gracious loving or life-giving acts. This is why the apostle Paul stated, "But of him are ye in Christ Jesus, who of God is made unto us wisdom, and righteousness, and sanctification, and redemption" (1 Cor. 1:30).

Righteousness is what God does for us and in us from within the sanctuary every day, and it is what is called the gospel of Jesus Christ or the gospel of the sanctuary, God abiding in the midst of His people to teach, reproof, correct, and instruct in truth and in spirit.

This complete ministry of God by His own and in us is the gospel of salvation, which equals the objective gospel and subjective gospel from His sanctuary. "The objective gospel is what God already has done for the human race in Christ Jesus, our Substitute, and the subjective gospel is what God does in the believer's life with those who have received Christ through the Holy Spirit before His coming" (E.H. 'Jack' Sequeira, *Fundamentals of the Everlasting Gospel*, p. 8).

The objective and subjective gospel are not a different gospel. It is the same righteousness of God for the human race or simply justification by faith as is stated in Romans 1:17, "The just shall live by faith."

Justification is the work of the sanctuary to free humankind from the bondage of Satan, sin, selfishness, and death and give us the eternal kingdom of God through the services of the courtyard, the holy place, and the Most Holy Place.

Ellen G. White explains it this way. Imputation ensures that you will enter the kingdom, and impartation fits you to enter the kingdom of God. So justification by faith is the true activity in the sanctuary. Justice is performed in the courtyard of the sanctuary of God where the innocent animals were killed for the sins of the people on a daily basis. The blood was then carried to the holy place for the cleansing, which was the type (indicator) of the antitype of Jesus Christ on the cross. The blood of Christ, with its everlasting cleansing power, once and for all saved us and made it unnecessary to ever sacrifice animal blood again.

This justification was earned by Jesus for the entire human race who believe in Christ and follow the instructions of the Holy Spirit (John 16:7-14). The entire work of atonement, reconciliation, righteousness, justification, sanctification, and redemption is to build the believers into the very character and nature of Jesus Christ. This naturalization and characterization is the mystery of the sanctuary system, the gospel of the everlasting good news for the human race. This unity of God with the believer helps Christians to grow into the perfection of the Father (Matt. 5:48) and the fullness of Jesus Christ (Eph. 4:19) through the guidance of the Holy Ghost unto all truth (John 16:13).

As we grow in Christ's character, we are automatically led to the very nature of Christ so that we can emulate Christ on earth in our daily lives. The real growth of Christ's nature in the believer's life truly manifests itself or reveals the life of Christ's humanity in the genuine understanding of the gospel of Jesus Christ and the gospel of the Sanctuary, which is the ministry of atonement, reconciliation, righteousness, wisdom, justification, sanctification, and redemption.

All these terms are summed up in the true character of Christ and the true growth of genuine Christianity. The character of Jesus equals a genuine Christian nature. The genuine Christian nature or genuine Christian growth is the true reflection of the object lesson of Christ in the Christian's life. Jesus said, "Let your light so shine before men, that they may see your good works, and glorify your Father which is in heaven" (Matt. 5:16).

The summation of the character of God and the nature of the genuine Christian is visible in Isaiah 11:2 which reads, "The spirit of the LORD shall rest upon him, the spirit of wisdom and understanding, the spirit of counsel and might, the spirit of knowledge and of the fear of the LORD."

These are seven characteristics of Christ that He lived by on this earth and set as our example. The apostle John wrote the following instruction as to our responsibilities as Christ's followers: "That they all may be one; as thou, Father, art in me, and I in thee, that they also may be one in us: that the world may believe that thou hast sent me. And the glory which thou gavest me I have given them; that they may be one, even as we are one: I in them, and thou in me, that they may be made perfect in one; and that the world may know that thou hast sent me, and hast loved them, as thou hast loved me" (John 17:21-23).

The seven characteristics of Christ are summed up with the glory of the Father that the Son shared or imparted to believers that the believers may reflect the same image and likeness of Jesus Christ to others.

The characteristics are described to certify the growth of genuine Christians in the truth of Christ that they may imitate Christ in their daily lives that the good news of God and the gospel of Jesus Christ may be seen. After a baby is born, it grows every day. So also the Christian grows in truth and in Spirit unceasingly.

23

First, the beginning of the knowledge of the Lord is the fear of the Lord. The word fear in this reference means to revere, worship, believe, accept, trust, and respect. Fear of the Lord is trusting Him, rejoicing in the goodness of the Lord, committing self to worship Him, and totally resting and waiting upon Him. This is the beginning of growth in the Lord (Ps. 37:2-7).

Second, the Spirit of knowledge is acquaintance, recognition, study, comprehension, appreciation, perception, learning, and teaching. Knowledge is the second stage of growth and a time when we study the Bible to determine who we are and where we came from. True comprehension of our creation, design, structure, image, and likeness leads us to recognize and appreciate God.

True spiritual knowledge frees us from the bondage of Satan, sin, selfishness (work of the flesh), the world, and the power of death. Without knowledge many people perish under the curse and dominion of Satan and sin (Hosea 4:6). A lack of growth in a spiritual knowledge of God affects families, communities, nations, and, at large, the world. Development of true knowledge involves learning and teaching. This kind of growth prepares us for the next level of growth.

Third, the Spirit of might (power) is the extension of the strong increase of knowledge. It is only through the power of the Spirit that believers can be successful physically, psychologically, emotionally, socially, culturally, economically, and spiritually. By choosing to trust in God and God alone, believers can be mighty and strong. When believers follow the direction of the Spirit with respect, reverence, and true knowledge, their success, prosperity, and achievements will be evident as they grow in Christ and mirror Him to those around them. As a believer's spiritual insight grows, God prepares them for the next stage of growth.

Fourth, when a Christian has grown in godliness by being persistent and consistent, then this person becomes a fellow member of the household of God. Such a fellowship with God guides Christians to be representatives or ambassadors of God on earth. Now the believer is royal member of God's kingdom and is set aside for the service of God on earth. God calls believers His children, co-rulers, heirs, and He calls us to be apostles, ministers, evangelists, teachers, elders, and deacons on this earth. Every believer is a representative of God as long as the believer is growing in God.

This is the interconnected growth of a Christian that leads to the higher level of confirmation and a trustworthy relationship with the Trinity.

Fifth, understanding is the stage of growth when the believer is considered upright in the sight of God such as Joseph, Job, Daniel, David, John the Baptist, Stephen, John the Revelator, and so many others whose names are recorded in the Bible and in the book of life. These believers went through the fiery furnaces to glorify the name of the eternal God.

The inseparable bond of man with God is one that compels the believer to be a shareholder of the household of God. Paul clearly states to us, "For through him we both have access by one Spirit unto the Father. Now therefore ye are no more strangers and foreigners, but fellowcitizens with the saints, and of the household of God; And are built upon the foundation of the apostles and prophets, Jesus Christ himself being the chief corner stone; In whom all the building fitly framed together groweth unto an holy temple in the Lord: In whom ye also builded together for an habitation of God through the Spirit" (Eph. 2:18-22).

This understanding bridges the next realm of critical growth of a Christian toward the character or nature of godliness.

Sixth, wisdom creates the power of discernment in the believer. The message of God in the life of a believer is the prophecy of God, translation of God, transcript of God, and the law of God. The real and true development of the spiritual character of God in the believer's life is his/her total association with God and humankind. This is the bond of an exceedingly developed spiritual personality of the believer. Wisdom is the beginning of the manifestation of the character of God personified in the believer's life. The apostle Paul considers this level as the ultimate stage of growth. In 1 Corinthians 1:30 he writes, "But of him are ye in Christ Jesus, who of God is made unto us wisdom, and righteousness, and sanctification, and redemption." This level of growth guides us to understand the final stage of a believer's growth.

Seventh, the final stage of the growth of a believer is what the apostles Paul and Peter dared to boldly declare and describe as the full growth of a Christian, one in which believers fully mirror their Creator. The following texts examine this philosophy:

"Knowing this, that our old man is crucified with him, that the body of sin might be destroyed, that henceforth we should not serve sin. For he that is dead is freed from sin. Now if we be dead with Christ, we believe that we shall also live with him: Knowing that Christ being raised from the dead dieth no more; death hath no more dominion over him. For in that he died, he died unto sin once: but in that he liveth, he liveth unto God. Likewise reckon ye also yourselves to be dead indeed unto sin, but alive unto God through Jesus Christ our Lord" (Rom. 6:6-11).

"I am crucified with Christ: nevertheless I live; yet not I, but Christ liveth in me: and the life which I now live in the flesh I live by the faith of the Son of God, who loved me, and gave himself for me" (Gal. 2:20).

"Whereby are given unto us exceeding great and precious promises: that by these ye might be partakers of the divine nature, having escaped the corruption that is in the world through lust" (2 Pet. 1:4).

"That we should be to the praise of his glory, who first trusted in Christ.... Which is the earnest of our inheritance until the redemption of the purchased possession, unto the praise of his glory.... That the God of our Lord Jesus Christ, the Father of glory, may give unto you the spirit of wisdom and revelation in the knowledge of him ... And what is the exceeding greatness of his power to us-ward who believe, according to the working of his mighty power ... Far above all principality, and power, and might, and dominion, and every name that is named, not only in this world, but also in that which is to come: And hath put all things under his feet, and gave him to be the head over all things to the church, Which is his body, the fullness of him that filleth all in all" (Eph. 1:12-23).

"And to know the love of Christ, which passeth knowledge, that ye might be filled with all the fulness of God. Now unto him that is able to do exceeding abundantly above all that we ask or think, according to the power that worketh in us" (Eph. 3:19, 20).

God manifested His character in the human race through His Son. His glory was among humankind, encouraging, teaching, and urging everyone to worship God in spirit and truth. God sought to reinstate humanity to its rightful place before the fall; that is the reason Christ died for us. Then the Holy Spirit came to earth on the day of Pentecost to guide us into all truth and lead humanity to God the Father. At that point, God the Father established His covenant relationship through the blood of His only Son. Thus, the Father imparted His glory to us through Christ Jesus.

Jesus Christ gave us His own life (body, soul, and spirit) that we may emulate His character and nature. The Father loves all humankind just as much as His own Son. But may I suggest that God the Father loves us more than His only Son. The reason I suggest this is because not one human being has ever tasted the death of the wages of sin. But there is one, the only Son, Jesus Christ, who tasted the wages of sin, which was the second death. The agape love of God, which unconditionally unites us to Him, is good news in regards to the gospel of the sanctuary or the abiding of God with humankind and humankind with God from now to eternal oneness or "atonement."

God's love for us is unfathomable, but once it fills us, we experience the fullness of God in our lives (Eph. 3:19). The character of Christ was developed as he grew from a child into a man. He took on our flesh, and in total harmony with His Father in heaven, he took on His character, setting an example for us to follow (Phil. 2:7).

If we want to develop the mind of Christ, we must allow the Spirit to lead us into all truths. We are called to be God's children, but we must surrender our will to His (Ps. 82:6; Room. 8:14-16). Romans 8:17 says, "And if children, then heirs; heirs of God, and joint-heirs with Christ; if so be that we suffer with him, that we may be also glorified together."

When we grow in Christ and make Him Lord of our lives, we are granted the honor of being His heir and we gladly agree to suffer for His name. Thus, we shun Satan, sin, and worldliness as we run toward the Light. At this stage of growth, the believer is fully reliant on God.

As a living sanctuary, Christ dwelt among us, and the Holy Spirit dwells in us. This living gospel of the sanctuary compels us to study and understand the redemptive act of God in the ancient sanctuary in the wilderness. We must also

27

study how we, as human beings, serve as the sanctuary on earth today, and the sanctuary looks like in heaven before and after Christ's second coming.

Chapter 3

God Dwelling in the Wilderness Sanctuary

This chapter does not seek to explain the pros and cons of God but to shed light on what is means when we reference God in the context of the sanctuary services of the wilderness, modern sanctuary on earth, and in the heavenly sanctuary before and after the second advent of Christ. The sanctuary ministry examines how God established His personal relationship with His people in the wilderness, how He is establishing that same relationship today, and how He will establish His covenant relationship with His people after Christ's return.

Wilderness Sanctuary

God personally spoke to Moses saying, "And let them make me a sanctuary; that I may dwell among them. According to all that I shew thee, after the pattern of the tabernacle, and the pattern of all the instruments thereof, even so shall ye make it" (Exod. 25:8, 9).

God was particularly involved in the affairs of His people after He freed them from Egypt, guiding, teaching, and protecting them with His immediate presence. This commitment of God had always been a part of His original plan of fellowshipping with the human race. Now God asked Moses and the people to pitch a tent for Him that would be adjacent to His peoples' tents. The amazing love of God was once again revealed in the wilderness. Besides walking with them at night with the pillar of fire, protecting them from the terror of darkness, He also was present in the pillar of the cloud during the day, protecting them from the scorching heat of the wilderness. In addition, he was in daily verbal communication with Moses and the priests.

God sought to nurse the children of Israel and raise them to maturity so that they could, in turn, teach other heathen nations to know God and worship Him, the true God rather than their gods, which idols made by people.

In order to do this, God had to reveal His glory in a direct and personal way by establishing a testimony of who He is, especially in reference to the Trinity. John expressed it this way in his Epistle: "For there are three that bear record in heaven, the Father, the Word, and the Holy Ghost: and these three are one. And there are three that bear witness in earth, the Spirit, and the water, and the blood: and these three agree in one" (1 John 5:7, 8).

The three persons of the Godhead have ways that blend and work together in an inter-related practice. God established the center of priestly services in the sanctuary with three divisions. These three divisions are the courtyard, the holy place, and the Most Holy Place, also known as the Holy of Holies. These sections are described as the place of sacrifice (courtyard), the place of ministry (holy place), and God's dwelling place (Most Holy Place).

Ordinary people were deeply afraid to approach God because of His exceedingly splendid glory. So God wanted to reveal Himself through His mercy seat in the Most Holy Place. As God revealed Himself through the services of the sanctuary, it was His desire that His people would know that they were safe. The acts of the priests were to be done under the direction of and with guidance from God Himself, serving as a foreshadow of the completeness of redemptions story in Jesus Christ.

> "And all the people saw the thunderings, and the lightnings, and the noise of the trumpet, and the mountain smoking: and when the people saw it, they removed, and stood afar off. And they said unto Moses, Speak thou with us, and we will hear: but let not God speak with us, lest we die. And Moses said unto the people, Fear not: for God is come to prove you, and that his fear may be before your faces, that ye sin not" (Exod. 20:18-20).

In order for the people to understand the importance of the sanctuary ministry, let this writing shed light on the significance of the services, locations, and objects in the sanctuary.

Locations or Divisions of Sanctuary

Wilderness	Earthly	Heavenly
Courtyard	**Body**	**Christ**
Holy Place	**Soul**	**Holy Ghost**
Most Holy Place	**Spirit**	**Father**

Look at how God's loving covenant relationship is interwoven throughout heaven and earth and how exceedingly great it is. It is so much more than the human mind will ever be able to comprehend. There is no way we can understand the sheer magnitude of His glory, but at the same time, He desires to simplify Himself so that He can approach us where we are and lift all those who choose to follow Him to His level.

The above comparative is to explain how the earthly and heavenly ministries of God work in the sanctuary and how the sanctuary is intertwined or connected with and uncontestable bond.

First, let us examine the ministry in the wilderness sanctuary and the furniture used in the sanctuary services.

Courtyard

This was an open space around the sacred tent, which contained the holy place and Most Holy Place and was surrounded by screens of fine linen suspended from or on pillars of brass. The entrance to this courtyard was closed with woven curtains of very expensive and glorious materials. The courtyard was only half of the height of the tabernacle so that the children of Israel could see who was performing the services.

At the entrance of the courtyard was the brazen altar of burnt offerings. Upon it all of the sacrifices were consumed by fire. The ashes were sprinkled with atoning blood. The laver, located between the altar and the door of the tabernacle, was made of brass and was used by the priests as a wash basin for their hands and feet before they entered the sacred compartments and approached the altar of burnt offering unto the Lord.

Holy Place

The table of shewbread, candlesticks, and the altar of incense were in the holy place. The table of shewbread was overlaid with pure gold, and each Sabbath the priests placed twelve cakes in two piles and sprinkled them with frankincense. The old ones were removed by the priests and replaced every Sabbath with fresh ones. The old ones had to be eaten by the priests since they were accounted as holy (Lev. 24:5-9).

"And thou shalt make a mercy seat of pure gold: two cubits and a half shall be the length thereof, and a cubit and a half the breadth thereof. And thou shalt make two cherubims of gold, of beaten work shalt thou make them, in the two ends of the mercy seat. And make one cherub on the one end, and the other cherub on the other end: even of the mercy seat shall ye make the cherubims on the two ends thereof. And the cherubims shall stretch forth their wings on high, covering the mercy seat with their wings, and their faces shall look one to another; toward the mercy seat shall the faces of the cherubims be

"And thou shalt put the mercy seat above upon the ark; and in the ark thou shalt put the testimony that I shall give thee. And there I will meet with thee, and I will commune with thee from above the mercy seat, from between the two cherubims which are upon the ark of the testimony, of all things which I will give thee in commandment unto the children of Israel.

"Thou shalt also make a table of shittim wood: two cubits shall be the length thereof, and a cubit the breadth thereof, and a cubit and a half the height thereof. And thou shalt overlay it with pure gold, and make thereto a crown of gold round about. And thou shalt make unto it a border of an hand breadth round about, and thou shalt make a golden crown to the border thereof round about. And thou shalt make for it four rings of gold, and put the rings in the four corners that are on the four feet thereof. Over against the border shall the rings be for places of the staves to bear the table. And thou shalt make the staves of shittim wood, and overlay them with gold, that the table may be borne with them. And thou shalt make the dishes thereof, and spoons thereof, and covers thereof, and bowls thereof, to cover withal: of pure gold shalt thou make them. And thou shalt set upon the table shewbread before me alway" (Exod. 25:17-30).

The shewbread represents Christ, the Bread of Life. It points to the Jesus, the Word of God, and the priests were to eat the "Word of God," the Scriptures. John wrote in the Scriptures, "Then Jesus said unto them, Verily, verily, I say unto you, Moses gave you not that bread from heaven; but my Father giveth you the true bread from heaven. For the bread of God is he which cometh down from heaven, and giveth life unto the world" (John 6:32, 33).

Candlestick

The candlestick of pure gold is described in Exodus 25:31-38:

"And thou shalt make a candlestick of pure gold: of beaten work shall the candlestick be made: his shaft, and his branches, his bowls, his knops, and his flowers, shall be of the same. And six branches shall come out of the sides of it; three branches of the candlestick out of the one side, and three branches of the candlestick out of the other side: Three bowls made like unto almonds, with a knop and a flower in one branch; and three bowls made like almonds in the other branch, with a knop and a flower: so in the six branches that come out of the candlestick. And in the candlestick shall be four bowls made like unto almonds, with their knops and their flowers.

"And there shall be a knop under two branches of the same, and a knop under two branches of the same, and a knop under two branches of the same, according to the six branches that proceed out of the candlestick. Their knops and their branches shall be of the same: all it shall be one beaten work of pure gold. And thou shalt make the seven lamps thereof: and they shall light the lamps thereof, that they may give light over against it. And the tongs thereof, and the snuffdishes thereof, shall be of pure gold."

The candlestick was to typify Christ, shining in fullness of the power of the Holy Spirit (Isa. 11:2; John 1:4, 9; Heb. 1:9; Rev. 1:4).

Jesus is the true Light for men, removing the darkness of Satan, sin, the world, self, and death. The seven-branched candlestick with its seven lamps was ornamental with accurately wrought flowers resembling lilies, which was made of one solid piece of pure gold. There were no windows in the tabernacle. The lamps were never extinguished at any time, but they shone by day and by night just as Christ is the light of life, always shining by day and by night.

Altar of Incense

Read Exodus 30:7-10 to learn more about the altar of incense:

"And Aaron shall burn thereon sweet incense every morning: when he dresseth the lamps, he shall burn incense upon it. And when Aaron lighteth the lamps at even, he shall burn incense upon it, a perpetual incense before the LORD throughout your generations. Ye shall offer no strange incense thereon, nor burnt sacrifice, nor meat offering; neither shall ye pour drink offering thereon. And Aaron shall make an atonement upon the horns of it once in a year with the blood of the sin offering of atonements: once in the year shall he make atonement upon it throughout your generations: it is most holy unto the LORD."

The main purpose of the altar of incense was to serve as a place for the priests to burn incense every morning and evening. There was to be perpetual incense before the Lord.

Most Holy Place

Read Exodus 25:10-22 to gain a better understanding or the ark that was the main feature in the Most Holy Place. This apartment was the center of the service for the atonement and intercession of sins. In the Most Holy Place, earth and heaven were connected. God's presence dwelt above the mercy seat, inside of which the Ten Commandments were laid.

The Ten Commandments are the basis of the covenant between God and His people. The connection between the Ten Commandments and the mercy seat is that God's kingdom is a kingdom of order and justice, and yet it is also full of mercy, kindness, and love. The mercy seat was structured from one solid piece of gold with two cherubim also made of gold on top of the mercy seat at the two ends. The cherubim stretched forth their wings, covering the mercy seat, and their faces looked at each other, slightly bent toward the mercy seat. In other words, the cherubim bowed down to look at the ark and the Ten Commandments with respect for the principle, order, and justice of the Creator. The law of God enshrined in the ark was the greatest principle of God's personal character, righteousness, and judgment.

Meanwhile, they also gave glory in worshipping God who revealed Himself at the mercy seat to redeem humankind. Cherubim always worship their Creator with their faces covered in humility and great respect. They give glory and offer continual praises for His Omnipotence, Omniscience, and Omnipresence. Above the mercy seat was the Shekinah or the manifestation of the very presence of the divine God between the cherubim where God made known His will and communed with the high priest on the Day of Atonement. When the light fell upon the right side of the cherubim, it signified God's acceptance and approval, but if a cloud rested on the left side of the cherubim, it revealed disapproval or rejection (*Spiritual Gifts,* vol. 4a, p. 102).

The psalmist states, "Mercy and truth are met together; righteousness and peace have kissed each other. Truth shall spring out of the earth; and righteousness shall look down from heaven.... Righteousness shall go before him; and shall set us in the way of his steps" (Ps. 85:10-13).

The Priest

Before the era of Abraham, every man was priest of his own family. Then afterward, from Abraham to Moses, the eldest son of the family was priest. From the time of Moses until the birth of Christ, the Levitical priesthood was systematized by the order and ordination of the tribe of Levi for the sanctuary services according to God's design. Aaron and the children of Aaron, which is the type of Christ Himself, were to serve in the sanctuary. After Christ's first advent, He became the true High Priest, standing as an eternal advocate on earth and in heaven.

"In accordance with their office, a special dress was appointed for the priests. 'Thou shalt make holy garments for Aaron thy brother for glory and for beauty," was the divine direction to Moses. The robe of the common priest was of white linen, and woven in one piece. It extended nearly to the feet and was confined about the waist by a white linen girdle embroidered in blue, purple, and red. A linen turban, or miter, completed his outer costume. Moses at the burning bush was directed to put off his sandals, for the ground whereon he stood was holy. So the priests were not to enter the sanctuary with shoes upon their feet" (*Patriarchs and Prophets,* p. 350).

While in the sanctuary service they were to take off their sandals and leave them in the courtyard. Then they were to wash their hands and feet before ministering in the sanctuary or placing a burnt offering on the altar of burnt offering. Particles on the sandals could defile or desecrate the holy place.

The garments of the high priest were more intricate and sacred than even the common priests for the special ministrations they were called upon to perform. "In addition to the linen dress of the common priest, he wore a robe of blue, also woven in one piece. Around the skirt it was ornamented with golden bells, and pomegranates of blue, purple, and scarlet. Outside of this was the ephod, a shorter garment of gold, blue, purple, scarlet, and white. It was confined with by a girdle of the same colors, beautifully wrought. The ephod was sleeveless, and on its gold-embroidered shoulder pieces were set two onyx stones, bearing the names of the twelve tribes of Israel.

"Over the ephod was the breastplate, the most sacred of the priestly vestments. This was of the same material as the ephod. It was in the form of a square, measuring a span, and was suspended from the shoulders by a cord of blue from golden rings. The border was formed of a variety of precious stones, the same that form the twelve foundations of the City of God" (*Patriarchs and Prophets,* p. 351).

On the borders of the breastplate were written the names of the twelve tribes of Israel. Aaron was told that he should bear the "names of the children of Israel in the breastplate of judgment upon his heart, when he goeth into the holy place for a memorial in front of the Lord continually" (Exod. 28:29). This is also an example of Christ, our High Priest, pleading with the Father and Holy Spirit on the sinner's behalf, bearing upon His heart the names of every repentant believer.

There are two brilliant stones on the right and left sides of the breastplate—Urim and Thummim. Urim means light or glory. Thummim means perfection of the sanctuary from the earthly to the heavenly. Through them the will or message of God was related to the high priest. "When questions were brought for decision before the Lord, a halo of light encircling the precious stone at the right was a token of the divine consent or approval, while a cloud shadowing the stone at the left was an evidence of denial or disapprobation" (*Patriarchs and Prophets,* p. 351).

The high priest's miter or turban was made of white linen and a blue and gold plate bore the inscription, "Holiness of Jehovah." Every piece of clothing and every act of the priests was to be of such as to demonstrate holiness and a sense of worship.

The services or ministrations in the sanctuary took place on a daily and annual basis. The daily ministration was done twice a day, once in the morning and again in the evening. The daily services occurred at the altar of burnt offering in the courtyard of the tabernacle and in the holy place. The high priest conducted the annual service once a year, which will be discussed in more detail later on in the book.

The daily ministration, which took place in the morning and evening, consisted of offering sweet incense on the golden altar and special offerings for individual sins. "Every morning and evening a lamb of a year old was burned upon the altar, with its appropriate meat offering, thus symbolizing the daily consecration of the nation to Jehovah, and their constant dependence upon the atoning blood of Christ" (*Patriarchs and Prophets,* p. 352).

Because the offering pointed to Christ, it had to be without blemish to show the perfection and purity of God's Lamb who would some day offer Himself for the sins of the human race (Exod. 12:5). Jesus was a "lamb without blemish and without spot" (1 Pet. 1:19). Paul repeats the same admonishment for the followers of Christ as was performed in the wilderness sanctuary by the instruction of God to Moses on Mount Sinai. "I beseech you therefore, brethren, by the mercies of God, that ye present your bodies a living sacrifice, holy, acceptable unto God, which is your reasonable service" (Rom. 12:1).

Those who have chosen Him as their personal Savior can't offer less than their best. The perfect and pure genuine service of their life pleases God the Father from heaven in the same manner as the Father said to His Son when He came out of the river after having been baptized in the Jordan: "And Jesus, when he was baptized, went up straightway out of the water: and, lo, the heavens were opened unto him, and he saw the Spirit of God descending like a dove, and lighting upon him: And lo a voice from heaven, saying, This is my beloved Son, in whom I am well pleased" (Matt. 3:16, 17).

By faith we can be pure and perfect children of God, which God Himself calls the "temple of God," the place where He abides (1 Cor. 3:16; 6:19, 20). Paul's message to the believer is this: "And the very God of peace sanctify you wholly; and I pray God your whole spirit and soul and body be preserved blameless unto the coming of our Lord Jesus Christ" (1 Thess. 5:23).

Just as the priests sacrificed a lamb each morning and evening, so must the believer's daily life also demonstrate the character of Christ as pure and perfect, following Jesus' earthly example.

The offering of incense in the morning and evening was burnt on the altar of incense in the holy place just before the entrance of the Most Holy Place. The smoke of the incense rose and God's divine glory descended upon the mercy seat and filled the Most Holy Place. By blood and the incense offering, God approached as the Mediator through whom repentant sinners could come to God and receive mercy and salvation. During the morning and evening sacrifice and incense services, worshipers assembled near the tabernacle and offered earnest prayers in confession of their sins.

The most important part of the daily services was the service performed on behalf of individuals. Sinners would bring a sin offering to the door of the tabernacle and place their hands upon the head of the sacrificial animal and confess their sins. The sin was then ceremonial transferred from the sinner to the innocent sacrifice. The sinner then killed the animal in the courtyard of the sanctuary, and the priest carried the blood to the holy place and sprinkled it before the veil, "behind which was the ark containing the law that the sinner had transgressed" (*Patriarchs and Prophets,* p. 354).

Ellen White goes on to say, "By this ceremony the sin was, through the blood, transferred in figure to the sanctuary. In some cases the blood was not taken into the holy place; but the flesh was then to be eaten by the priest, as Moses directed the sons of Aaron, saying, 'God hath given it you to bear the iniquity of the congregation' Leviticus 10:17" (*Patriarchs and Prophets,* p. 355).

When a sin offering was presented for a priest and the congregation, the blood was carried into the holy place and sprinkled before the veil and placed upon the horns of the altar. The fat was consumed or burned upon the altar of burnt offering in the courtyard, but the body of the sacrifice was burned outside of the camp (Lev. 4:21).

However, when the sacrifice was offered for a ruler or for one of the people, the blood was placed on the horns of the altar of burnt offering and poured out at the bottom of it (Lev. 4:22-35).

There was also a special ceremony needed for the removal of the sins. God established an annual ceremony when sin for the entire congregation had to be removed from the sanctuary. This ceremony was known as the Day of Atonement. This was an annual cleansing of sin from the sanctuary and a removal of the sins of the repentant sinner. This act points to the second coming of Christ when all sins will be forever wiped clean.

On the Day of Atonement, the high priest entered into the Most Holy Place to complete the yearly ministration of services to cleanse the sanctuary. It was on this day that two kid goats "were brought to the door of the tabernacle, and lots were cast upon them, 'one lot for the Lord, and the other lot for the scapegoat.' The goat upon which the first lot fell was to be slain as a sin offering or sacrifice for the people. And the priest was to bring his blood within the veil, and sprinkle it upon the mercy seat" (*Patriarchs and Prophets,* p. 355). The blood of the sacrifice was sprinkled upon the altar of incense, the veil of the holy place, and finally, upon the mercy seat to atone for the sins and transgressions of the children of Israel.

Then the high priest would come out of the Most Holy Place and stand at the door of the tabernacle. "And Aaron shall lay both his hands upon the head of the live goat, and confess over him all the iniquities of the children of Israel, and all their transgressions in all their sins, putting them upon the head of the goat, and shall send him away by the hand of a fit man into the wilderness: And the goat shall bear upon him all their iniquities unto a land not inhabited: and he shall let go the goat in the wilderness" (Lev. 16:21).

Until the scapegoat, a live goat, was sent away from the camp, the congregation was not free from their sins. Therefore, the children of Israel were to pray, fast, and search their hearts while the atonement work was taking place.

"Important truths concerning the atonement were taught the people by this yearly service. In the sin offerings presented during the year, a substitute had been accepted in the sinner's stead; but the blood of the victim had not made full atonement for the sin. It had only provided a means by which the sin was transferred to the sanctuary. By the offering of blood, the sinner acknowledged the authority of the law, confessed the guilt of his transgression, and expressed his faith in Him who was to take away the sin of the world; but he was not entirely released from the condemnation of the law. On the Day of Atonement the high priest, having taken an offering for the congregation, went into the most holy place with the blood and sprinkled it upon the mercy seat, above the tables of the law" (*Patriarchs and Prophets,* p. 356).

Ellen White continues, "Thus the claims of the law, which demanded the life of the sinner, were satisfied. Then in his character of mediator the priest took the sins upon himself, and, leaving the sanctuary, he bore with him the burden of Israel's guilt. At the door of the tabernacle he laid his hands upon the head of the scapegoat and confessed over him 'all the iniquities of children of Israel, and all their transgressions in all their sins, putting them upon the head of the goat.' And as the goat bearing these sins was sent away, they were, with him, regarded as forever separated from the people. Such was the service performed 'unto the example and shadow of heavenly things' Hebrews 8:5" (*Patriarchs and Prophets,* p. 356).

The scapegoat represents Satan who, at the end of time, will carry the iniquities of the whole human race. Sins will forever be vanished from existence, and believers in Christ will be separated from Satan and death. We will then be united with the Father, Son, and Holy Spirit. The saints and the host of holy angels will dwell together in harmony for eternity.

The connection of the sanctuary in the wilderness with the modern or earthly sanctuary and the heavenly sanctuary after the second advent of Christ basically has the same central theme or motif in regards to the covenant relationship with God and His people. In the next chapter, we will explore the modern or earthly sanctuary to shed more light on how it plays out as a very important part to link both the sanctuary ministry of the wilderness sanctuary to the heavenly sanctuary ministry.

Chapter 4

God's Work in the Modern or Earthly Sanctuary

The same Omnipotent, Omniscient, Omnipresent one who spoke with Moses, abided in the wilderness sanctuary, and is working in the heavenly sanctuary still abides in the modern or earthly sanctuary today.

The amazing truth of the sanctuary manifested in the wilderness is manifested in person through the earthly sanctuary of today. To establish the truth of this concept, we need to look to Scripture and read God's directives to His people regarding their role as the temple of the Holy Spirit. In the wilderness God dwelt among His people in the tabernacle, but when Jesus returned to heaven after His resurrection, He sent the Holy Spirit to dwell in and among His people.

The apostle Paul was one of the greatest writers of the gospel of Jesus Christ. He extensively and explicitly elaborated about the modern sanctuary on earth, which is the believer: "Know ye not that ye are the temple of God, and that the Spirit of God dwelleth in you? If any man defile the temple of God, him shall God destroy; for the temple of God is holy, which temple ye are" (1 Cor. 3:16, 17).

God is simply saying to you that you are the temple of God. With emphatic repetition, the text is directly addressing each of us. God through Paul is saying that we are all the temple of God, and the Spirit of God dwells in us.

Further in 1 Corinthians, Paul again brings up this point. "What? know ye not that your body is the temple of the Holy Ghost which is in you, which ye have of God, and ye are not your own? For ye are bought with a price:

therefore glorify God in your body, and in your spirit, which are God's" (1 Cor. 6:19, 20). This text is even clearer as to the role of our body serving as the temple of the Holy Ghost.

Now let's look at Galatians 2:20: "I am crucified with Christ: nevertheless I live; yet not I, but Christ liveth in me: and the life which I now live in the flesh I live by the faith of the Son of God, who loved me, and gave himself for me."

This text clearly states that Paul was alive and was no longer living by himself. Christ was residing in Paul's life and was shaping Paul's character and daily life by living within him just as God living among His people in the wilderness sanctuary. This is the same God who daily manifested Himself in the life of Paul.

Turn now to 2 Peter 1:4: "Whereby are given unto us exceeding great and precious promises: that by these ye might be partakers of the divine nature, having escaped the corruption that is in the world through lust." The wilderness sanctuary was to be free from blemishes or sin; so also, we must be blameless from lust and corruption as Christians, as representatives of God.

"For this is the covenant that I will make with the house of Israel after those days, saith the Lord; I will put my laws into their mind, and write them in their hearts: and I will be to them a God, and they shall be to me a people" (Heb. 8:10). Just as God placed the Ten Commandments in the ark in the Most Holy Place in the wilderness sanctuary, so also He places His law in the mind and heart of His people as a living example of the modern earthly sanctuary. This verse opens the door to a clearer understanding of the relationship or similarity of the wilderness sanctuary with the modern earthly sanctuary in human beings.

God's law was penned by His own finger and preserved in the Most Holy Place as part of the old covenant between God and the children of Israel. Now, during the new covenant era, God's law is written in each believer's heart and mind, and the Holy Spirit dwells within us (1 Cor. 3:16, 17; 6:19, 20).

While subject to the old covenant, God promised that the ministry of the sanctuary in the wilderness would be transferred from the wooden temple to human beings.

"But this shall be the covenant that I will make with the house of Israel; After those days, saith the LORD, I will put my law in their inward

42

parts, and write it in their hearts; and will be their God, and they shall be my people. And they shall teach no more every man his neighbour, and every man his brother, saying, Know the LORD: for they shall all know me, from the least of them unto the greatest of them, saith the LORD: for I will forgive their iniquity, and I will remember their sin no more" (Jer. 31:33, 34).

"A new heart also will I give you, and a new spirit will I put within you: and I will take away the stony heart out of your flesh, and I will give you an heart of flesh. And I will put my spirit within you, and cause you to walk in my statutes, and ye shall keep my judgments, and do them" (Ezek. 36:26, 27).

These scriptures definitely point to God connecting the wilderness sanctuary ministry of the old covenant with the human temple ministry of the modern earthly sanctuary even before the apostles were born or began to write. The indwelling of God in human beings was imminent in the heart and mind of God. His covenant relationship toward humankind was and is immeasurable and incomprehensive. It is exceedingly above all that can be eternal, timeless, real, true, experiential, and everlasting.

The reason Christ was born and took on the full responsibility of the wages of sin was to transfer the sanctuary ministration of the wilderness from the wooden temple to the human temple. After His baptism, at which time the Father acknowledged his Son and the Holy Spirit descended on Him as a dove, Jesus worked, taught, healed, evangelized, and shepherded His disciples. After His crucifixion, resurrection, and ascension, the Holy Spirit descended from heaven in the form of tongues of fire on the day of Pentecost.

It was after this that the apostle Paul emphatically wrote, "And what agreement hath the temple of God with idols? for ye are the temple of the living God; as God hath said, I will dwell in them, and walk in them; and I will be their God, and they shall be my people" (2 Cor. 6:16).

Here again, Paul openly declares that genuine believers are the temple of the living God in whom He dwells in and walks with. Paul reminds Christians that they must understand the doctrine of the sanctuary. It is imperative because the sanctuary is the utmost and only doctrine that envelops the entire doctrine

43

of the redemption story.

"For this is the covenant that I will make with the house of Israel after those days, saith the Lord; I will put my laws into their mind, and write them in their hearts: and I will be to them a God, and they shall be to me a people: And they shall not teach every man his neighbour, and every man his brother, saying, Know the Lord: for all shall know me, from the least to the greatest. For I will be merciful to their unrighteousness, and their sins and their iniquities will I remember no more. In that he saith, A new covenant, he hath made the first old. Now that which decayeth and waxeth old is ready to vanish away" (Heb. 8:10-13).

In this text it concludes that He destroyed the old wilderness system at the cross, which was signified by the veil in the temple that was torn from top to bottom (Matt. 27:51; Mark 15:37; Luke 23:45).

Now, on earth without a doubt mentions of the indwelling place, the abiding place, or the temple references the Holy Spirit dwelling within Christ's followers, who He has set aside to be blameless in His sight and through His saving grace (1 Thess. 5:23). But if we, as Christians, are to be the temple of God, we must be a holy and living sacrifice that is acceptable to God, not conforming to the world but rather being transformed by the renewing of own mind that we may prove what is the good, acceptable, and perfect will of God in us by the very grace and mercies of Jesus who escaped from the corruption of the world (Rom. 12:1, 2; 2 Pet. 1:4).

In order to understand more clearly the modern earthly sanctuary's ministration in comparison with the wilderness sanctuary, the following pages are devoted in particular to comparing the division, location, purposes, significant services, representations, and implications of the sanctuary.

Structural Comparison

Wilderness Sanctuary	Human Sanctuary
Courtyard	Body
Holy Place	Soul
Most Holy Place	Spirit

Courtyard Services

The courtyard in the wilderness sanctuary functioned as the place of the daily sacrifice for the forgiveness of sin. The courtyard was a place where justice could be sought and found.

After sinners placed their hands on the sacrifice, confessed their sins, and killed the animal and the priest sprinkled the blood of the sacrifice on the curtain of the holy place, the sin was ceremonially transferred to the sanctuary and held their until the Day of Atonement. On that day the sin was blotted from the sinner.

The courtyard was where the congregation waited for forgiveness every day when the priest came to the sanctuary for both the morning and evening's burnt offerings. The congregation would pray for forgiveness, seeking justice from God for their transgressions.

All who came by faith to the courtyard received forgiveness because of the presence of God in the sanctuary and the sacrificial blood that was offered on their behalf. As they witnessed the sacrificial offering, sinners were impressed with the fact that God did not excuse sin, in fact, sin separated humanity from God, but He provided a way of forgiveness.

Unlike the character of God, sin is a defect; it is impure. All of the courtyard activities were to resemble or symbolize the coming Messiah. Jesus lived a perfect life and was crucified on the cross for all our sins. Innocent, pure, perfect, and godly, Christ died on behalf of sinners. The courtyard is the most demonstrative disclosure of Christ's mission.

The events that took place in the courtyard were open for all to see. Similarly, everyone was witness to Jesus' crucifixion. The redemptive act of Jesus Christ was open for all to see. Jerusalem's inhabitants were witness to the innocent victim, Jesus, being slain for the sins of all who transgress the law of God. Jesus, the innocent Lamb, was offered as a sacrifice for human sin.

Jesus was judged by the highest Judge in the cosmic world—God the Father— whose law was violated by humanity for which God demands justice. The wages of sin were paid on the cross on our behalf. The demand of the law was only then fully met. The prince of this world rejoiced in the murder of Jesus, yet his time would come (Isa. 14:12-15; Rev. 12:7-9).

Justice and mercy met together on the cross to cover the sin of sinners. Because of Jesus' sacrifice, the price was paid for the penalty of breaking the law, and in turn, God offers eternal mercy to anyone who accepts Jesus Christ as their personal Savior (John 3:16; Rom. 6:23; Gal. 3:13; Phil. 2:8; Rev. 20:6).

The courtyard service was to expose the sinners' transgression of the law of God and for the sinner to recognize his or her need of forgiveness from God. The innocent animal that was slain in offering for the sin pointed to Christ who was also innocent and never committed any sin—He became sin in place of the sinner, forever paying for the sins of the world and setting all believers free. This is the service that was exposed in the courtyard.

To conclude, the courtyard services depicted the physical birth, growth, lifestyle, ministry, crucifixion, resurrection, and ascension of Christ in experience, truth, reality, and personal practice on earth. By going through all of this, Christ paid the wages of sin once and for all and vindicated Himself against Satan's false accusations that God is a tyrant. "Forasmuch then as the children are partakers of flesh and blood, he also himself likewise took part of the same; that through death he might destroy him that had the power of death, that is, the devil; And deliver them who through fear of death were all their lifetime subject to bondage" (Heb. 2:14, 15).

Holy Place Services

After the courtyard service, the priest carried on with a service in the holy place twice a day, after the morning and evening sacrifices.

The priest would burn sweet incense on a daily basis, thereby symbolizing the daily need of consecration for the entire nation of Israel to God and their constant dependence upon the atoning blood of Christ.

Paul and Peter, respectively, confirmed this through their messages when it was said, "I beseech you therefore, brethren, by the mercies of God, that ye present your bodies a living sacrifice, holy, acceptable unto God, which is your reasonable service" (Rom. 12:1), and "But with the precious blood of Christ, as of a lamb without blemish and without spot: Who verily was foreordained before the foundation of the world, but was manifest in these last times for you" (1 Pet. 1:19).

In the holy place the priestly rites were to sprinkle the blood and prepare the sweet incense offering. After the morning and evening sacrifices, the priest would carry the blood from the courtyard to the holy place and sprinkle the blood on the golden altar before the veil that separated the holy place from the Most Holy Place, which housed the ark containing the Ten Commandments that the sinner had transgressed against. This ceremony took place every day.

On some occasions, a meat offering was eaten by the priest and the priest would go into the holy place instead of sprinkling the blood. The meat offering that the priest ate was mostly for rulers or people of authority (Lev. 4:22-35; 6:26; 10). Whether the sacrifice involved the sprinkling of blood or the eating of the meat, the sin of the congregation was ceremonially transferred to the holy place.

"In the offering of incense the priest was brought more directly into the presence of God than in any other act of the daily ministration. As the inner veil of the sanctuary did not extend to the top of the building, the glory of God, which was manifested above the mercy seat, was partially visible from the first apartment. When the priest offered incense before the Lord, he looked toward the ark; and as the cloud of incense arose, the divine glory descended upon the mercy seat and filled the most holy place, and often so filled both apartments that the priest was obliged to retire to the door of the tabernacle. As in that typical service the priest looked by faith to the mercy seat which he could not see, so the people of God are now to direct their prayers to Christ, their great High Priest, who, unseen by human vision, is pleading in their behalf in the sanctuary above

"The incense, ascending with the prayers of Israel, represents the merits and intercession of Christ, His perfect righteousness, which through faith is imputed to His people, and which can alone make the worship of sinful beings acceptable to God. Before the veil of the most holy place was an altar of perpetual intercession, before the holy, an altar of continual atonement. By blood and by incense God was to be approached—symbols pointing to the great Mediator, through whom sinners may approach Jehovah, and through whom alone mercy and salvation can be granted to the repentant, believing soul" (*Patriarchs and Prophets,* p. 353).

It was while the incense was burning on the golden altar and the daily sacrifice was taking place that the congregation gathered and engaged in earnest confession of sin and prayers. The congregation assembled in the courtyard and would unite with the priests in silent prayer as they faced the holy place, hoping in faith that their petitions ascended to God with the smoke and that they could receive forgiveness of sin and God's abundant blessings for their life.

Within the holy place was also the shewbread. Each Sabbath the priest brought twelve loaves of fresh bread to place on the table. Six loaves of bread were stacked in two columns. This signified that the children of Israel were to depend upon God for both their physical and spiritual sustenance.

Israel's livelihood daily depended on their Creator, Deliverer, and Redeemer. This shewbread was also a part of the daily sacrifice. Frankincense was placed upon the loaves, and when the shewbread was replaced the next Sabbath with fresh loaves, the frankincense was burned upon the golden altar as a memorial before God. The shewbread was a symbol of Christ: "I am the living bread which came down from heaven" (John 6:51).

Moving on to the next piece of furniture in the holy place, the seven lamps made of one solid piece of gold were lit by the serving priest and shone continually, both day and night, without being extinguished. The functional reason behind this was because the holy place and Most Holy Place were without windows. Only fresh-squeezed or pressed oil was used in the golden candlestick to light the holy place—the Shekinah glory of God from the mercy seat shone in the Most Holy Place and lighted that area.

The candlestick symbolized Christ who is the eternal Light of the world (John 1:4; 8:12). In the wilderness, God appeared in the pillar of fire, providing light for the Israelites all night long. And at the beginning of time, God created light (Gen. 1:4, 5). From the first day of Creation until the fourth day, God served as the natural light of Creation until He made the sun, moon, and stars (Gen. 1:3).

The light of the candlesticks and the Shekinah glory pointed to God's presence with His people. God pitched His tent by their tents to protect them from physical and spiritual darkness.

As we've discussed, the importance of the holy place services is that the sin of the sinner was transferred from the sinner to the priest and then the priest carried it to the sanctuary and the sin was then transferred into the holy place until the Day of Atonement in the Most Holy Place or Holy of Holies.

The sinner was temporarily freed until the Day of Atonement when the sin of the entire congregation was placed upon the head the scapegoat, therefore, representing total separation of sin from individuals as well as the congregation on an annual basis.

Most Holy Place Services

God directed Moses to instruct Aaron that the sanctuary services were to be conducted to teach the children of Israel the error of their ways and the saving grace of God. Israel, whom He had brought out of slavery, was to serve Him and be His representative to the nations around them.

God cannot have any kind of relationship with any kind or form of sin. God is sinless. He wants His people to be free from sin in order for them to have a personal relationship with Him as His bride.

The sanctuary service was to restore God's chosen people, who had been freed from physical slavery in Egypt, from the slavery of sin. The people of Israel were physically, mentally, psychologically, socially, culturally, economically, and spiritually bankrupt after centuries of hardships at the hand of tyranny under the rule of Pharaoh and Satan. God wanted to restore the nation of Israel and use them to be His messengers as a model people of His righteousness and holiness and partakers of His life.

"Therefore, behold, I will allure her, and bring her into the wilderness, and speak comfortably unto her.... And I will betroth thee unto me for ever; yea, I will betroth thee unto me in righteousness, and in judgment, and in lovingkindness, and in mercies. I will even betroth thee unto me in faithfulness: and thou shalt know the LORD" (Hosea 2:14-20).

The entire purpose of the sanctuary was to help God build a genuine loving covenant relationship forever with His people on this earth. The main reason God called Israel out of the land of slavery, which represented Satan who oppressed Israel and stripped their freedom of worship so that Pharaoh, or Satan, could enforce heathen beliefs and practices on the Israelites, was to develop the nation as ambassadors for Him.

Those who refused to practice heathenism in Egypt were sentenced to death or imprisoned for life with harsh physical punishment and back-breaking manual labor until they died.

Our merciful and loving God with His righteous mighty hand plucked them out from under Pharaoh and freed them to worship the living and everlasting God who created the heavens and the earth along with the vast universe.

Since His glory would consume His creation, He had to dwell among them through the sanctuary. God chose to pitch His sanctuary in the midst of His people in spite of the wickedness of humanity. He systematized the sanctuary service in its merciful path, pointing His children to the true Redeemer who would come to eliminate sin. God particularly implemented the annual atonement service in the sanctuary ministry to signify the end of sin, which kept the human race under the bondage of tormenting fear.

The service of the Most Holy Place was the breakthrough reconciliation system of God toward humankind. God's covenant relationship is similar to that of a husband or wife who loves their spouse and stays committed to them even though the spouse has committed adultery and been unfaithful to the marriage relationship. God's relationship is an everlasting, merciful, loving one, although we are unlovable and unacceptable. Fortunately, He still builds a relationship with unfaithful cheats and seeks to bestow righteousness on the sinner, and then He treats our enmity with love.

This kind of self-sacrificing love is the character and lifestyle of God. The truthfulness of God has been present from the beginning. God created humanity in His personal image and likeness and gave us the breath of life. After the fall He instituted a plan to save humankind and restore His creation to our original glory.

Despite sin, God pursued a living covenant relationship with humanity. He built a relationship with the patriarchs, such as Adam, Abel, Noah, Abraham, Moses, and Joshua; the prophets; the apostles, and today's Christians.

His faithfulness endures forever. He is worthy to be trusted at every cost because of His graciousness and willingness to share with us His heritage and the hope of glory. His covenant was first extended to Israel but was extended to everyone with His death on the cross.

Therefore, God established the sanctuary system in the wilderness and ordained its practices until Christ's death on the cross, at which time the ceremonial service was no longer necessary. After Christ's ministry the sanctuary service system transferred to human beings and the heavenly sanctuary ministry to Jesus, our High Priest who became human and purchased humanity by his own blood. The human life and heavenly sanctuary system will be explained in detail in the latter sections of this book.

Let's continue to look at the Most Holy Place's service to uncover more light to understand clearly what God did for His people.

The importance of the Most Holy Place in the sanctuary was to manifest God's glory and for mercy to be granted to the people. On an annual basis, the high priest entered the Most Holy Place to cleanse the sanctuary.

Two goats were brought to the door of the tabernacle. Lots were cast for them: "one lot for the LORD, and the other lot for the scapegoat" (Lev. 16:8).

God commanded His people to perform the ordinance in this way: "And he shall make an atonement for the holy place, because of the uncleanness of the children of Israel, and because of their transgressions in all their sins: and so shall he do for the tabernacle of the congregation, that remaineth among them in the midst of their uncleanness.... And he shall sprinkle of the blood upon it with his finger seven times, and cleanse it, and hallow it from the uncleanness of the children of Israel" (Lev. 16:16, 19).

The goat that the lot fell upon for the LORD was sacrificed as the sin offering for the people. The priest carried the blood from the courtyard to within the veil and sprinkled it directly on the mercy seat over the law to make satisfaction for the requirement of the law of God. Then the blood was also sprinkled upon the altar of incense that was before the veil.

After that the high priest came out from the Most Holy Place through holy place to the courtyard and the waiting congregation. The high priest would then lay both hands upon the head of After putting this on the head of the scapegoat, a fit man led the live goat into the wilderness. Now, the scapegoat took all the iniquities of the congregation into the uninhabited land (Lev. 16:21, 22).

The scapegoat could not come back to the Israelites camp. This was done to openly declare before the congregation just how much God abhors sin. Even the person who took the scapegoat out to the uninhabited land had to go through some special cleansing before officially being allowed back into camp. The person had to wash himself and his clothing with water before joining the camp. This system was set up by God to mark the holiness of God, His abhorrence of sin, and the fact that, once atoned, the children of Israel should never again come in contact with or be polluted by the sin.

Every Israelites was to afflict their souls during the atonement process. All the businesses of Israel were required to shut down. All of Israel was responsible for praying and fasting with humility during this time to afflict their souls and to show God their loyalty and to receive forgiveness for all of the iniquities committed throughout the year.

Now, Christ is the only High Priest for the heavenly sanctuary and for the earthly temple of the human body (1 Cor. 3:16). This profoundly explains the complete authority of the priesthood of Christ in both the earthly and heavenly sanctuaries. "And what is the exceeding greatness of his power to us-ward who believe, according to the working of his mighty power, Which he wrought in Christ, when he raised him from the dead, and set him at his own right hand in the heavenly places, Far above all principality, and power, and might, and dominion, and every name that is named, not only in this world, but also in that which is to come: And hath put all things under his feet, and gave him to be the head over all things to the church, Which is his body, the fullness of him that filleth all in all" (Eph. 1:19-23).

The point here is to certify that Jesus is the only High Priest in both the church body on earth and the temple ministration in the holy place and Most Holy Place in the heavenly sanctuary today.

Christ is the only head of the heavenly sanctuary and earthly Christian church body. This scriptural verification clarifies the true nature of the modern earthly sanctuary's reality, which is not built in stone or with wooden but rather is the human body.

The wilderness sanctuary was constructed of three parts in the pattern of the heavenly sanctuary, which was not built by human hands, but by God's own hand. The wilderness sanctuary was framed from gold and wood, but the human temple is structured from life and body, or physical and spiritual. Also, the wilderness sanctuary was made up of the courtyard, holy place, and Most Holy Place ministries. So also the human temple or sanctuary is framed in a format of three. The three sections of the human temple or sanctuary are body, soul, and spirit.

In order to achieve true understanding of the human temple or sanctuary clearly, it is best to verify it from the Scriptures. The following scriptures are a selection of the many that will shed light on the subject.

Human beings are constituted from three very important elements—the spirit, soul, and body are inseparable entities. "And the very God of peace sanctify you wholly; and I pray God your whole spirit and soul and body be preserved blameless unto the coming of our Lord Jesus Christ" (1 Thess. 5:23). Now, let's describe these individually in order to better understand what is being said.

Spirit

Humankind is made of the spirit, which is declared in God's Word: "And God said, Let us make man in our image, after our likeness: and let them have dominion over the fish of the sea, and over the fowl of the air, and over the cattle, and over all the earth, and over every creeping thing that creepeth upon the earth" (Gen. 1:26). God Himself is Spirit. God is a Spirit—"God is a Spirit: and they that worship him must worship him in spirit and in truth" (John 4:24).

That is one of the major reasons that even some non-believers of God the Father, Son, and Holy Spirit attempt to worship some form of god. The majority of the world's religions are based around some form of worship, whether that worship takes place in temples, shrines, churches, or mosques. There are millions and billions who are still seeking someone who can be greater than themselves, who can protect them from some kind of immediate catastrophe when it arises. Even some atheists seek to find out if there is a big bang theory that is greater than them because they are still searching for something.

Let us read a number of different texts and discover what God has to say about this in the Scriptures:

> "And God said, Let us make man in our image, after our likeness: and let them have dominion over the fish of the sea, and over the fowl of the air, and over the cattle, and over all the earth, and over every creeping thing that creepeth upon the earth" (Gen. 1:26).

"And they told him all the words of Joseph, which he had said unto them: and when he saw the wagons which Joseph had sent to carry him, the spirit of Jacob their father revived" (Gen. 45:27).

"And they came, every one whose heart stirred him up, and every one whom his spirit made willing, and they brought the LORD's offering to the work of the tabernacle of the congregation, and for all his service, and for the holy garments" (Exod. 35:21).

"But Sihon king of Heshbon would not let us pass by him: for the LORD thy God hardened his spirit, and made his heart obstinate, that he might deliver him into thy hand, as appeareth this day" (Deut. 2:30).

"And it came to pass, when all the kings of the Amorites, which were on the side of Jordan westward, and all the kings of the Canaanites, which were by the sea, heard that the LORD had dried up the waters of Jordan from before the children of Israel, until we were passed over, that their heart melted, neither was there spirit in them any more, because of the children of Israel" (Josh. 5:1).

"But God clave an hollow place that was in the jaw, and there came water thereout; and when he had drunk, his spirit came again, and he revived: wherefore he called the name thereof Enhakkore, which is in Lehi unto this day" (Judg. 15:19).

"He that hath no rule over his own spirit is like a city that is broken down, and without walls" (Prov. 25:28).

"And Hannah answered and said, No, my lord, I am a woman of a sorrowful spirit: I have drunk neither wine nor strong drink, but have poured out my soul before the LORD" (1 Sam. 1:15).

"But Jezebel his wife came to him, and said unto him, Why is thy spirit so sad, that thou eatest no bread?" (1 Kings 21:5).

"And the God of Israel stirred up the spirit of Pul king of Assyria, and the spirit of Tilgathpilneser king of Assyria, and he carried them away, even the Reubenites, and the Gadites, and the half tribe of Manasseh, and brought them unto Halah, and Habor, and Hara, and to the river Gozan, unto this day" (1 Chron. 5:26).

"Now in the first year of Cyrus king of Persia, that the word of the LORD spoken by the mouth of Jeremiah might be accomplished, the LORD stirred up the spirit of Cyrus king of Persia, that he made a proclamation throughout all his kingdom, and put it also in writing" (2 Chron. 36:22).

"Therefore I will not refrain my mouth; I will speak in the anguish of my spirit; I will complain in the bitterness of my soul" (Job 7:11).

"Thou hast granted me life and favour, and thy visitation hath preserved my spirit" (Job 10:12).

"Into thine hand I commit my spirit: thou hast redeemed me, O LORD God of truth" (Ps. 31:5).

"The LORD is nigh unto them that are of a broken heart; and saveth such as be of a contrite spirit" (Ps. 34:18).

"I call to remembrance my song in the night: I commune with mine own heart: and my spirit made diligent search" (Ps. 77:6).

"When my spirit was overwhelmed within me, then thou knewest my path. In the way wherein I walked have they privily laid a snare for me" (Ps. 142:3).

"Hear me speedily, O LORD: my spirit faileth: hide not thy face from me, lest I be like unto them that go down into the pit" (Ps. 143:7).

"A talebearer revealeth secrets: but he that is of a faithful spirit concealeth the matter" (Prov. 11:13).

"The spirit of a man will sustain his infirmity; but a wounded spirit who can bear?" (Prov. 18:14).

"The spirit of man is the candle of the LORD, searching all the inward parts of the belly" (Prov. 20:27).

"The burden of the word of the LORD for Israel, saith the LORD, which stretcheth forth the heavens, and layeth the foundation of the earth, and formeth the spirit of man within him" (Zech. 12:1).

"For what man knoweth the things of a man, save the spirit of man which is in him? even so the things of God knoweth no man, but the Spirit of God" (1 Cor. 2:11).

"The Spirit itself beareth witness with our spirit, that we are the children of God" (Rom. 8:16).

By no means should the spirit be confused with the Holy Spirit, breath of life, soul, human being, or person. The spirit of a person is one of the most important components of the three elements that make up a human being. This portion or component is extremely important to make humanity different from all of the other animals in God's creation. This is the main reason that humankind worships or looks for a superior power over themselves who can protect them from immediate danger or destruction. Even atheists want protection and seek or invent heavy weaponry to replace God. Therefore, every person is made of the *spirit, soul, and body.* The spirit of man is the innermost part or the conscious in every man.

If the believer of God or the converted man's spirit is his innermost part, then the conscious is the dwelling place of God that lies in the human spirit. Within the believer, the spirit can be compared with the Most Holy Place of the sanctuary, which was the chamber of the Most High.

Isaiah 57:15 says, "For thus saith the high and lofty One that inhabiteth eternity, whose name is Holy; I dwell in the high and holy place, with him also that is of a contrite and humble spirit, to revive the spirit of the humble, and to revive the heart of the contrite ones." This text declares that God dwells in the spirit of the believer. God cannot inhabit a non-believer. Why? Because the non-believer does not accept or allow God to dwell within him or her. If a believer is a temple of God, then God can reveal Himself within the innermost part of the believer, which is the spirit of the person. The very indwelling Spirit of God causes a believer to worship God and then the believer's spirit is the seat of God's will.

Once God dwells in the spirit of a human being, the believer is a new creation. The new birth experience of the believer causes a believer to produce the character of God, which leads to holiness and sanctification. The indwelling Spirit of God in the believer's life is the imputing of God, the grace of God or the righteousness of God.

The apostle Paul states it as this, "I am crucified with Christ: nevertheless I live; yet not I, but Christ liveth in me: and the life which I now live in the flesh I live by the faith of the Son of God, who loved me, and gave himself for me" (Gal. 2:20).

The indwelling of God in the believer frees the believer from Satan, sin, the world, self, and death. What God does without or apart from a man is called justification (imputation), and what God does in the Christian's life is called sanctification (impartation), which is a Christian's journey in the character of Christ or walking in the Spirit. (Gal. 5:16).

When a Christian is regenerated by the Holy Spirit, the Christian begins to walk in the light of life. The Christian is free from the bondage of sin. A Spirit-controlled life produces service that pleases God in their everyday life. A Christian who is free from the bondage of sin is someone who walks in the light. That is why Jesus told His disciples, "Ye are the light of the world" (Matt. 5:14), the world that doesn't know Jesus, the true Light of the world. The Spirit of the converted believer represents the Most Holy Place.

In the old covenant, the law was written on the tables of stone and placed within the ark. In the new covenant, the law is written in the heart of converted Christians and placed in the innermost part of the spirit of a person.

Jeremiah 31:33 tells us, "But this shall be the covenant that I will make with the house of Israel; After those days, saith the LORD, I will put my law in their inward parts, and write it in their hearts; and will be their God, and they shall be my people." Also, Ezekiel 36:27 says, "And I will put my spirit within you, and cause you to walk in my statutes, and ye shall keep my judgments, and do them."

Turning to the New Testament, we find the following about the covenant. "For this is the covenant that I will make with the house of Israel after those days, saith the Lord; I will put my laws into their mind, and write them in their hearts: and I will be to them a God, and they shall be to me a people" (Heb. 8:10).

What is the relationship between the law and the sanctuary of God? The following brief description helps to answer that question. The importance of the law for the humanity is outlined in Psalm 119:97-105: "O how love I thy law! it is my meditation all the day. Thou through thy commandments hast made me wiser than mine enemies: for they are ever with me. I have more understanding than all my teachers: for thy testimonies are my meditation. I understand more than the ancients, because I keep thy precepts. I have, refrained my feet from every evil way, that I might keep thy word. I have not departed from thy judgments: for thou hast taught me. How sweet are thy words unto my taste! yea, sweeter than honey to my mouth! Through thy precepts I get understanding: therefore I hate every false way. Thy word is a lamp unto my feet; and a light unto my path."

Joshua 1:7-9 says, "Only be thou strong and very courageous, that thou mayest observe to do according to all the law, which Moses my servant commanded thee: turn not from it to the right hand or to the left, that thou mayest prosper whithersoever thou goest. This book of the law shall not depart out of thy mouth: but thou shall meditate therein day and night, that thou mayest observe to do according to all that is written therein: for then thou shall make thy way prospereous, and then thou shalt have good success. Have not I commanded thee? Be strong and of a good courage: be not afraid, neither be thou dismayed: for the LORD thy God is with thee whithersoever thou goest."

And in Psalm 1:2, 3, it says, "But his delight in the law of the LORD; and in his law doth he meditate day and night. And he shall be like a tree planted by the rivers of water, that bringeth forth his fruit in his season; his leaf also shall not wither; and whatsoever he doeth shall prosper."

The law of the Lord—God's commandments—is the true source and foundation of wisdom, understanding, strength, prosperity, and everlasting joy—it is "sweeter also than honey and the honeycomb (Ps. 19:10). If the law of the Lord is that important, then there is no reason that any person should not respectfully fall in love with it.

When Jesus came to this earth to establish the law (Matt. 5:17-19), someone asked Jesus, "Master, which is the great commandment in the law? Jesus said unto him, Thou shalt love the Lord thy God with all thy heart, and with all thy soul, and with all thy mind. This is the first and great commandment. And the second is like unto it, Thou shalt love thy neighbour as thyself. On these two commandments hang all the law and the prophets" (Matt. 22:36-40).

The greatest law is to love each other and to love God with our spirit, soul, and body. Here, God is clearly calling all people to rest with God and in God. When God created all creation, He made man on the last day, the sixth day, and God called Adam and Eve to rest on the Sabbath, the seventh day and their first day in existence.

"And God said, Let us make man in our image, after our likeness: and let them have dominion over the fish of the sea, and over the fowl of the air, and over the cattle, and over all the earth, and over every creeping thing that creepeth upon the earth. So God created man in his own image, in the image of God created he him; male and female created he them.... And the evening and the morning were the sixth day. Thus the heavens and the earth were finished, and all the host of them. And on the seventh day God ended his work which he had made; and he rested on the seventh day from all his work which he had made. And God blessed the seventh day, and sanctified it: because that in it he had rested from all his work which God created and made" (Gen. 1:26-2:3).

Reader, you can see that man was created on the sixth day and entered new life with rest, not work. Adam and Eve did not contribute anything to the act of Creation. And even after the fall, humanity has contributed nothing for their redemption. The same God who created human beings for rest, not for toil, redeemed the human race for rest, not for self-redemption or self-righteousness. Christ said, "come unto me, all ye that labour and are heavy laden, and I will give you rest.... and ye shall find rest unto your souls" (Matt. 11:28, 29).

At Creation human beings were created to rest with God on the Sabbath. So also, God invites humanity to rest from sinful restlessness to restfulness in Christ. Humanity cannot contribute anything for their redemption—God's divine activities can only be performed by Him. Paul gives very strong counsel to all people: "For it is God which worketh in you both to will and to do of his good pleasure. Do all things without murmurings and disputings: That ye may be blameless and harmless, the sons of God, without rebuke, in the midst of a crooked and perverse nation, among whom ye shine as lights in the world" (Phil. 2:13-15).

Here God strongly counsels us that God's will can only be performed for His good pleasure by Him alone through us in the midst of the crooked world to magnify His glory. When God, by His merciful hand, called Israel out from the midst of the wicked nation of Egypt after 400 years of slavery, the Israelites contributed nothing to their freedom; they simply obeyed and were delivered. So God brought the nation that was called by His name out of bondage in hopes of protecting, guiding, correcting, and teaching them true godliness.

While in the wilderness, God gave them the Ten Commandments to teach them who He was and how they should live their lives for Him. The Ten Commandments reveal the everlasting character of God's omnipotence, omniscience, and omnipresence.

"And God spake all these words, saying, I am the LORD thy God, which have brought thee out of the land of Egypt, out of the house of bondage" (Exod. 20:1, 2). In this first commandment, God is saying, "I am the only God. I am the one who freed you with a mighty hand from the tyrannical rule of Pharaoh and the oppression of the cruel bondage or slavery. I freed you to know me as your God. I am the only *living* God, the life-giving Creator of the universe, the Redeemer and Savior of the world. No man or image or any creation is God, only Me."

The second commandment says, "Thou shalt have no other gods before me. Thou shalt not make unto thee any graven image, or any likeness of any thing that is in heaven above, or that is in the earth beneath, or that is in the water under the earth. Thou shalt not bow down thyself to them, nor serve them: For I the LORD thy God am a jealous God, visiting the iniquity of the fathers upon the children unto the third and fourth generation of them that hate me. And shewing mercy unto thousands of them that love me, and keep my commandments" (verses 4-6).

This law states that no one and nothing in creation can even serve as a substitute for the only Creator of the universe (Gen. 1:26; Matt. 28:19; 2 Cor. 13:14; 1 John 5:7-9). All other gods are dead gods, and people who worship other gods will face the judgment of the God of heaven. The true God—the Father, the Son, and the Holy Spirit—is indivisible and is worthy to be worshiped.

The third commandment says, "Thou shalt not take the name of the LORD thy God in vain; for the LORD will not hold him guiltless that taketh his name in vain!" (Exod. 20:7). This commandment states that no one should insult, mock, or disgrace the name of God. If someone does take the name of the Lord in vain, their punishment will be severe unless that person confesses the sin and pleads for the mercy and lovingkindness of the Lord. God deserves to be respected and honored and worshiped.

The fourth commandment says, "Remember the sabbath day, to keep it holy. Six days shalt thou labour, and do all thy work: But the seventh day is the sabbath of the LORD thy God: in it thou shalt not do any work, thou, nor thy son, nor thy daughter, thy manservant, nor thy maidservant, nor thy cattle, nor thy stranger that is within thy gates: For in six days the LORD made heaven and earth, the sea, and all that in them is, and rested the seventh day: wherefore the LORD blessed the sabbath day, and hallowed it" (verses 8-11).

The word "remember" means it is not new but has already existed or been known. Yes, Sabbath is the first law from Creation (Gen. 2:1-3). This is an exceedingly important text in the Bible because of its link to Creation and God's provision to His children. In this commandment God is calling people to come and rest with Him so that He can make their joy complete. He promises to give us rest from all our toil and the tumult of our daily lives. God is inviting believers with tenderness to come to Him for protection from the hand of Satan, sin, self, the world, and death. He says, "Come to me. I want to build an everlasting covenant relationship with you."

"He that dwelleth in the secret place of the most High shall abide under the shadow of the Almighty" (Ps. 91:1). This invitation of God is to make us His own glory as His own children because we are born of Him. "I have said, Ye are gods; and all of you are children of the most High" (Ps. 82:6). God loves His own more than Himself. God revealed His love on the cross by giving Himself for us. This same love drove God to establish His law around His love. The Sabbath is the foundation of the Ten Commandments. All the rest of the nine commandments are enveloped in Sabbath truth.

How is that possible? The very reason is that a person who is born of God and is rested in Him doesn't have any other gods. Doesn't worship any images, likenesses, nature, any other person, or angels. A person rested in God doesn't insult or take the name of God in vain. Believers rested in or with God can't abuse or disrespect their parents or any other human being, God, or angels. A person of God honors, respects, and treats others with kindness. A genuine believer won't kill, commit adultery, steal, bear false witness against anyone, or covet their neighbor's house, wife, or belongings. The Sabbath is the balancing and centering gravity of all the law. Please refer to the diagram of the Sabbath.

The fifth commandment says, "Honour thy father and thy mother: that thy days may be long upon the land which the LORD thy God giveth thee" (Exod. 20:12). Treat other as God treats you and them, with dignity, self-sacrificing love, and respect. They are created in the image of God and His likeness, just like you are. They are precious in His eyes.

The sixth commandment says, "Thou shalt not kill" (verse 13). Don't harm anyone in any way, physically, psychologically, emotionally, socially, culturally, economically, or spiritually, because human beings are an expressed image, likeness, and partaker of the divine breath and life of God (Gen. 1:26; 2:7; 2 Peter 1:2). God is the giver of life. No one has any right to take another person's life, for everyone belongs to God (1 Cor. 3:16, 17; 6:19, 20).

The seventh commandment says, "Thou shalt not commit adultery" (Exod. 20:14). Illicit sex is totally unacceptable in the sight of God. It is abhorrent. God is the one who established marriage between female and male. God created one person for another as husband and wife. Any illicit activities outside of a marriage relationship are unacceptable in the sight of God.

The eighth commandment say, "Thou shalt not steal" (Exod. 20:15). Do not take what doesn't belong to you. God is able to give us ample gifts of more than we can imagine if we believe that God is the giver of all heavenly riches. Those who steal are not blessed because they have harmed others.

The ninth commandment says, "Thou shalt not bear false witness against thy neighbour" (Exod. 20:16). Jesus clearly explains this statement in

Matthew 7:12: "Therefore all things whatsoever ye would that men could do to you, do ye even so to them: for this is the law and the prophets." In other words, don't lie. Don't harm or hurt anybody by lying. Everyone deserves to be treated fairly and honestly.

Finally, the tenth commandment says, "Thou shalt not covet thy neighbour's house, thou shalt not covet thy neighbour's wife, nor his manservant, nor his maidservant, nor his ox, nor his ass, nor any thing that is thy neighbor's" (Exod. 20:17). Don't be selfish. God, in His infinite wisdom, knew that seeking too much stuff adds stress to life. Instead of seeking earthly possessions, we should be seeking after God.

The law of God is a litmus test for believers in God who are waiting for the second coming of Christ. "Here is the patience of the saints: here are they that keep the commandments of God, and the faith of Jesus" (Rev. 14:12). The law of God is God's own words, decrees, and principles of His nature, which point to His character. Christ is our righteousness. Christ is our wisdom. He is our sanctification and our redemption. Christ is the embodiment of the law (1 Cor. 1:30). "For Christ is the end of the law for righteousness to every one that believeth" (Rom. 10:4). Christ is God. God Himself is the law. Therefore, the law of God is the most important foundation of wisdom, understanding, strength, counsel, prosperity, everlasting joy and success, and knowledge. If the law of God is the foundation of everything, the law of God is God Himself.

The law of God was placed in the Most Holy Place in the sanctuary where God revealed Himself through the Shekinah glory. The Ten Commandments were placed in the ark in the wilderness sanctuary because the law is holy. God's law was, is, and will be holy because God is holy. All men and women are unholy because of sin. In order to keep God's holy law, people must have God in their lives so that God's character can shine through the person.

When Moses returned from spending forty days and fortys night on Mount Sinai, Moses was glowing after being in the very presence of God. As I said before, the Ten Commandments are a transcript of God's nature or character. That is why God's law is an immutable principle and precept as Christ clearly stated in Matthew 5:17-19. God and His law are inseparable. God's law is His righteousness. His righteousness is His mercy, kindness, and love. God is merciful, kind, and loving. His law is His love. Love produces only love.

THE SABBATH

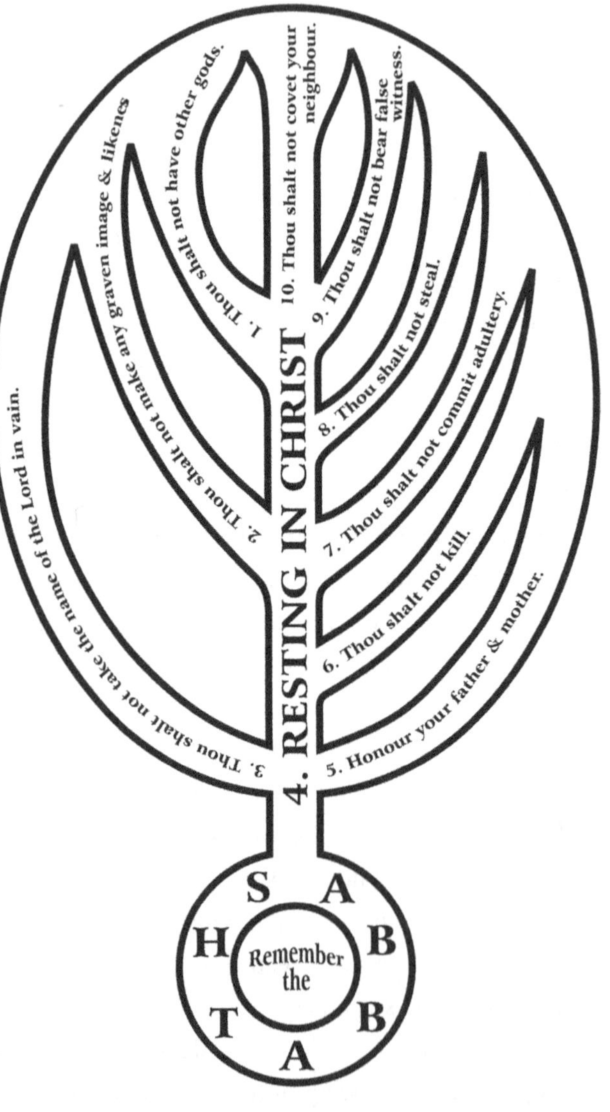
1. Thou shalt not have other gods.
2. Thou shalt not make any graven image & likenes
3. Thou shalt not take the name of the Lord in vain.
4. RESTING IN CHRIST
5. Honour your father & mother.
6. Thou shalt not kill.
7. Thou shalt not commit adultery.
8. Thou shalt not steal.
9. Thou shalt not bear false witness.
10. Thou shalt not covet your neighbour.
SABBATH
Remember the

Meaning of True Rest (Shabbbath Shalom)

A) Is it resting in self-opinion?
B) Is it resting on the people?
C) Is it resting on the day, or
D) Is it resting in Christ?

Fig.1

This is the main reason God's law was in the Most Holy Place where God was seated on the mercy seat of judgment. His judgment is a judgment of mercy, truth, love, kindness, faithfulness, humility, self-control, peace, and patience. These are fruits of the Holy Spirit. The spirit produces the spiritual fruits (Rom. 7:14).

God's law is a reflection of God's own character or nature. Review these characteristics in light of each commandment.

1. God is Creator, Sustainer, Redeemer, and Immortal.
2. God is a living God, not an idol.
3. God is glorious, honorable, and worthy of worship.
4. God is rest, peace, joy, kindness, gentleness, merciful, patient, faithful, truthful, and love.
5. God embodies respect, dignity, and integrity, giving it freely to all
6. God is the Life-giver.
7. God is the creator of holy marriage between one male and one female.
8. God is the giver of everything. He opens heaven doors for those who knock in holiness and selflessness.
9. God is the only Way, the Truth, and the Life. There is nothing false about Him.
10. God is the giver of good gifts. With all the money in the world at his disposal, He freely gives. He is a totally unselfish God.

This is the principle of the sanctuary of God that He was performing in His wilderness sanctuary in the Most Holy Place. When the wilderness sanctuary ministry ceased with Christ's death on the cross, the ministry was transferred directly to His creation. Human beings, those who believe in the redemption of Christ from Satan, sin, self, the world, and death, are the earthly temple or sanctuary (1 Cor. 3:16, 17; 6:19, 20; 2 Cor. 6:16; Eph. 2:21, 22) and the law of God is written in their heart, spirit, and inner person (Heb. 10:16; Jer. 31:33).

Christ came to this earth to bring unity between God and humankind as the Lamb of sacrifice, thus bringing rest to everyone who accepts His free gift. When God created Adam and Eve, He quickly introduced them to the blessed and holy (sanctified) Sabbath rest on the seventh day of Creation after forming the entire universe (Gen. 2:1-3). So when Christ came to redeem humanity, Christ called everyone to rest in Him and His Father. That is why Christ is our Sabbath rest. When we follow the law of God, we find rest and peace in Jesus our Redeemer.

Anyone who truly rests in Christ Jesus won't worship dead god or create images, likenesses, or idols to bow down to. No one in Christ can insult or disgrace or defile or take the name of God in vain or curse God. A rested person in Christ Jesus doesn't insult their mother and father. Nor could they kill another person. A person who is rested in Christ is an advocate for life. They don't commit adultery, steal, or witness falsely against their neighbors or anyone else. And they won't covet their neighbor's property or anyone else's things. Therefore, resting in Christ is a true foundation for our redemption and a basis for keeping the law of God. Indeed, Christ is the end of the law or a fulfillment of the law of God. Christ is love, and He demonstrated who God is and what God's law, which reveals His character, is like. The following diagram further explains these ideas.

Resting in Christ Jesus is resting on the Sabbath. The Sabbath is the law, and the law is the Sabbath. If anyone hates, breaks, dislikes, or separates the commandments, they are transgressors of the law. Christ is not in them. "For whosoever shall keep the whole law, and yet offend in one point, he is guilty of all" (James 2:10). They are considered lawbreakers, but those who keep the law of the Lord will enter the city of God having the right to the tree of life. Read what the apostle John was ordained to write concerning those who keep the law of God and who break the law of Christ. "I am Alpha and Omega, the beginning and the end, the first and the last. Blessed are they that do His commandments, that they may have right to the tree of life, and may enter in through the gates into the city. For without are dogs, and sorcerers, and whoremongers, and murderers, and idolaters, and whosesoever loveth and maketh a lie" (Rev. 22:13-15).

John received this message directly from the mouth of Christ who was John's Lord, Master, Friend, and Redeemer. Let God help us not to be the type of people John describes in verse 15. But those who rested on the Sabbath will be children of God who have the right to the tree of life, and they will enter the city of God. Resting on the Sabbath is resting in Christ Jesus, which produces total harmony or reconciliation with God vertically and with humankind horizontally. It is total rest of man in spirit, soul and body. This is the righteousness of Christ.

Accepting Sabbath rest and following all ten commandments is so important. Many so-called conservative Christians or believers teach against their own Savior in whom they believe is their personal Redeemer. Matthew 5:17-19 teaches us that Jesus did not change anything in the law and He said that anyone who breaks a commandment, even one, "shall be called the least in the kingdom of heaven."

Anyone who ignorantly or intentionally breaks God's law or teaches the traditions of human beings instead of God's laws will be responsible for their own personal destruction, exactly like Satan and his followers who were cast out of heaven, and will not be able to partake of the tree of life (Rev. 22:13-15). This is the law of Christ, and Christ Himself declared this truth. My prayer is that may all listen to the admonition of God today and prepare themselves to enter the city of God and have a right to the tree of life and be called children of God by the mercy and the grace of faith in Christ Jesus. I hope to see you in the morning of jubilee. Shalom!

In the aforementioned scriptures, it is verified that God's law is written in the heart and kept in the spirit of human beings where God reveals Himself with the Shekinah glory. The heart of man is an example of the ark of God and the spirit of the Most Holy Place. The Shekinah glory is the very glory with which God was, is, and will be the Light of the world.

"And whether we be afflicted, it is for your consolation and salvation, which is effectual in the enduring of the same sufferings which we also suffer: or whether we be comforted, it is for your consolation and salvation" (2 Cor. 1:6).

God chose to manifest Himself through the innermost part of us by sending the Holy Spirit to dwell in us. In the same manner, God dwelt in the Most Holy Place over the mercy seat in the wilderness. His Shekinah glory shone where no natural light could penetrate into the sanctuary because there were no windows. But in the Most Holy Place, the Shekinah glory illuminated the entire compartments of the holy place and Most Holy Place.

So also, the mercy seat represents the spirit of conversion in the Christian's spirit, the ark represents the heart of the converted Christian where the law of God is written. Christians, thereby, are the light to this dark and unbelieving world.

A converted life becomes changed and reflects God in character like the lives of Abel, Noah, Abraham, Joseph, Moses, Joshua, Samuel, Elijah, Elisha,

Ruth, Esther, Isaiah, Jeremiah, Ezekiel, Daniel and his friends, all of the prophets, all of the apostles, the Christians who were persecuted throughout the ages for the sake of the gospel, Ellen G. White, and missionaries who suffered much for the sake of the gospel of Jesus Christ.

The apostle Paul profoundly and clearly states, "The Spirit itself beareth witness with our spirit, that we are the children of God" (Rom. 8:16). The apostle's testimony is the true witness because he met Jesus face to face, personally, and then under the inspiration of God. The Holy Spirit, who dwelt in the life of Paul, told the apostle Paul that it was He who also dwelt in Jesus Christ (Gal. 2:20; Col. 2:9; Eph. 1:23; 3:19; 1 Cor. 3:16; 6:19, 20).

These texts profoundly describe or explain the indwelling of the Trinity within the human sanctuary of all Christians. Just as God's Shekinah glory shone forth from the wilderness sanctuary, so also does He continue to glorify Himself in the lives of believers, shining through the human life.

For this reason Jesus told the disciples, "Ye are the light of the world. A city that is set on an hill cannot be hid.... Let your light so shine before men, that they may see your good works, and glorify your Father which is in heaven" (Matt. 5:14, 16).

The amazing thing is that the Shekinah glory only appeared to the high priest once in a year, but the Shekinah glory was always in the Most Holy Place because the very presence of God was over the mercy seat and it is now in the human spirit and is manifested every day.

This same glory was glorified in Christ's life and was spoken of by Christ to His disciples, "And the glory which thou gavest me I have given them; that they may be one, even as we are one" (John 17:22).

The same light that shone from Jesus can shine today from the genuine Christian life. God's glory is God's character, which means that God's character is God's own immutable nature. Human beings who genuinely believes in God's creation, redemption, resurrection, and second advent of Christ are literally indwelt by the very nature of God.

Again, we have testimony by one of the apostles. The apostle Peter testified in this manner, "Whereby are given unto us exceeding great and precious promises: that by these ye might be partakers of the divine nature, having escaped the corruption that is in the world through lust" (2 Pet. 1:4).

The descriptive nature of God's abiding in the spirit of the believer certainly makes the believer the sanctuary, tabernacle (old covenant), or temple (new covenant). The nature of a believer having been given the very spirit, wisdom, might, knowledge, fear (reverence) of God points to the sanctuary relationship of the Christian with God (Isa. 11:2).

To make complete a human person as the sanctuary, let me give you a brief acknowledgement as to the root of these two components of a human being's soul and body.

The life of the converted Christian is led by the Holy Spirit because the converted Christian's spirit is the seat of God's Spirit (1 Cor. 3:16; 6:19, 20; Rom. 8:2).

The Holy Spirit-led Christian is fully controlled by Him. This controls the work of the soul, and in turn, the soul controls the body. Therefore, the believer who is converted does the work of God and doesn't do his or her own will. Persons possessed by the Holy Ghost surrender their own will to the will of God. This doesn't mean they are under the work of their own impulses; instead, all of the impulses are controlled by the will of God. Every impulse abhors the works of sin because sin separates self from every nature of the work of God.

The lives of genuine Christians glorify God with their whole person, consisting of their spirit, soul, and body. These individuals reflect the character of God the Father, the Son, and the Holy Spirit, objectively recognizing what God has done through His exceedingly great sacrifice to redeem humankind on the cross through His Son and subjectively what God does through Christ Jesus and the Holy Spirit by manifesting His own character through a genuine Christian life.

This kind of obedience prepares the genuine Christian to enter the kingdom of God. It makes the Christian a member of the household of God. God Himself certifies through the testimonies in scripture.

The Christians who reflect God's character are the "kings and priests" of God's household (Rev. 1:5, 6), co-regents (rulers) with Christ (Rom. 8:17), branches of God (John 15:4, 5), apples of His eye (Zech. 2:8), and ambassadors of God (2 Cor. 5:18-20). They are also engraved on the palms of the Lord God (Isa. 49:16),

God pitched His tent near the tents of the Israelites. Now, God pitches His tent, or temple, within the hearts of His followers. God was with human beings in the old covenant, but in the new covenant God moved into the human heart and spirit of those that ask Him to come in. God was in the Most Holy Place, and it was there that He communicated with the priest on the Day of Atonement. In the same pattern, God through His Son, Jesus Christ, manifested Himself in the human spirit through the Holy Spirit that Christians would love the righteousness of God and hate sin. "Be ye therefore perfect, even as your Father which is in heaven is perfect" (Matt. 5:48).

Forerunner Commentary has this to say, "The Hebrew word rendered 'blameless' (NKJV) or 'perfect' (KJV) in Genesis 17:1 means 'entire, complete, full, without blemish.' The Greek word found in Matthew 5:48 translated 'perfect' means 'finished, complete, having reached its end,' and implies being fully grown or mature. The definition of the English word *perfect* is 'lacking nothing essential to the whole, without defect, complete.' All three definitions contain the word 'complete.'"

There isn't any reason genuine believer can't grow in the fullness of God and reach spiritual maturity, or perfection. God, in His own fullness, resides in the believer's life. It is true that the genuine believer is perfect or complete in God.

Soul

Human beings are not only made up of their spirit, they are also made up of their soul and body. The soul is what makes the person a being. There are some scriptural facts that support this view; they are as follows:

"And Abram took Sarai his wife, and Lot his brother's son, and all their substance that they had gathered, and the souls that they had gotten in Haran; and they went forth to go into the land of Canaan; and into the land of Canaan they came" (Gen. 12:5).

"And the king of Sodom said unto Abram, Give me the persons, and take the goods to thyself" (Gen. 14:21).

"All the souls that came with Jacob into Egypt, which came out of his loins, besides Jacob's sons' wives, all the souls were threescore and six" (Gen. 46:26).

"And all the souls that came out of the loins of Jacob were seventy souls: for Joseph was in Egypt already" (Exod. 1:5).

"Thy fathers went down into Egypt with threescore and ten persons; and now the LORD thy God hath made thee as the stars of heaven for multitude" (Deut. 10:22).

"Then they that gladly received his word were baptized: and the same day there were added unto them about three thousand souls" (Acts 2:41).

"Then sent Joseph, and called his father Jacob to him, and all his kindred, threescore and fifteen souls" (Acts 7:14).

"Let every soul be subject unto the higher powers. For there is no power but of God: the powers that be are ordained of God" (Rom. 13:1).

"Which sometime were disobedient, when once the longsuffering of God waited in the days of Noah, while the ark was a preparing, wherein few, that is, eight souls were saved by water" (1 Pet. 3:20).

The aforementioned texts distinctively point out that the soul is referred to as a person(s). The reason being is that the throne and the entity (nature) of man's individuality or character is found in the soul.

From this point on the soul must be looked upon as Spirit-soul-body. As we established, man is constituted of spirit-soul-body (1 Thess.5:23). Now we will explain soul in context of the sanctuary ministry compared with the holy place in the wilderness and the Holy Spirit of the heavenly sanctuary.

These natures are mind (will, soul, memory) (Job 7:15), knowledge (Prov. 2:10; 19:2), and emotions (2 Sam. 5:8; Job 10:21; John 12:27). These are the ones that make up a person's personality. Every activity originates from the soul. The soul is the entity of the human self; it is the natural life. Because the soul is in control of the everyday functionality of humanity and is, in other words, the service center, it is equated as the holy place of the wilderness sanctuary of the converted believer.

The human soul is where all thoughts, desires, opinions, and feelings are produced. All of these products generate from the soul, which can be identified as self will. Self produces its own likeness or type. The point here is that the soul, or self, can only produce selfish things. The soul also automatically controls the body. The behavior of the body is determined by the work of the soul or self in the non-believer's activities. In other words, the converted believer's soul is controlled by the Holy Spirit who lives in the converted believer's spirit as was discussed previously.

In an unconverted person's life, the work of the soul is polluted by human selfishness and independence. When people became self-sufficient, they are becoming independent. When humankind is independent, people say, "I don't need anyone beside me, myself, and I." But people who say this are independent from God and make themselves their own creator. God calls it iniquity, which was started in the mind of Lucifer in heaven.

Iniquity means bending toward oneself. The turning toward oneself or your own way in the scriptures is wickedness. Now, the whole thing is wrapped up with self-seeking. Self-seeking is looking for self-glory, self-exaltation, and self-gratification. Thus the natural person (soul) can't make God rejoice. The natural person or unbeliever only seeks self-satisfaction. There is no sanctification in the natural person, because he or she only seeks self-fame and self-glorification.

Self-dependency is one of the things that caused Lucifer to be totally separated from God. Lucifer felt that he was above God. Lucifer felt that he could overthrow God. The scriptures reveal this wickedness as iniquity.

> "How art thou fallen from heaven, O Lucifer, son of the morning! how art thou cut down to the ground, which didst weaken the nations! For thou hast said in thine heart, I will ascend into heaven, I will exalt my throne above the stars of God: I will sit also upon the mount of the congregation, in the sides of the north: I will ascend above the heights of the clouds; I will be like the most High. Yet thou shalt be brought down to hell, to the sides of the pit." (Isa. 14:12-15).

Lucifer's ugly self revealed itself in front of creation. His ugly self kept repeating "I, I, I, I, I" will be like the Most High. That is what self does. The natural self, or soul, is very selfish and focused on me, myself, and I. The difference between the work of the soul in the believer and the non-believer is in the principle.

The principle of the unbeliever is "me, myself, and I," but for the believer the principle is "not I, but God and Him alone." The work of the life of self is unpleasing to God. It never agrees with God; it is totally contrary or in opposition with the principles of God. So it is totally unacceptable in the sight of God. It is contradictory to the work of the kingdom of God. The self-principle stands against the work of the sanctuary ministry in the human life. Therefore, the self-principle or the works of self belong to death. That is why Christ came to give His innocent life in place of the human race because no one else could deny self and save the world: "For all have sinned, and come short of the glory of God" (Rom. 3:23).

Christ brought all of self's activities to an end with His death on the cross. Only when self is relinquished in the soul does the soul become the partaker of the divine nature that is the sanctuary or temple of God. Otherwise, humanity cannot be the center of the ministry of God in the human sanctuary. The sinful, selfish mind of iniquity cannot serve God at all. Self must be completely silent in, with, and through death forever in order for the individual or church to be the temple of God or the center of the ministration that the world may be illumined once and for all before the second advent of Christ to rescue this miserably dying world.

In order to do that, believers must be awakened from the deadliness of denominational controversy and see the hope of the coming of Christ for personal and for the church's deliverance from the hand of the enemy—the devil.

Once the believer accepts by faith what Paul discovered—"I am crucified with Christ: nevertheless I live; yet not I, but Christ liveth in me: and the life which I now live in the flesh I live by the faith of the Son of God, who loved me, and gave himself for me" (Gal. 2:20)—a new dedication revives the individual or church of God. It does not defend self and does not hide any longer self-deception. It is then that the Holy Spirit conducts the believer's spirit, and in turn, the spiritual conscience conducts the soul. The soul in turn conducts the body and behaviors of the body according to the command of God's Spirit. The sanctified soul, which is the subject of the ministry of God, can be smoothly or harmoniously accomplished for the reconciliation or atonement vertically with God and horizontally with human beings on this earth. Then the glory of the gospel will be the hope of all who accept it.

When self is dead, God takes over. When, by faith, self is done away with, then the Spirit of God dwells within. Where God manifested Himself in the Most Holy Place and conducted the redemptive work in the holy place for His people. So the same pattern takes place from the dwelling of God in the spirit of human beings to the daily redemptive act that is performed through the soul (mind).

The most important work of forgiveness of sin of the transgressor of the law was daily performed in the holy place. The activities were described before in the section on the holy place of the wilderness sanctuary. The transgressor brought a sin offering of an innocent animal in place of their own self, and then the transgressor laid both hands on the animal and slew the animal in the courtyard. The blood of the sacrifice was carried by the priest to the holy place and sprinkled on the significant objects in the holy place. Then the action of forgiveness took place through the Urim and Thummim where the will of God was made known to the priest by a glorious light shining on the right side of the stone to indicate approval or agreement or with a shadowing of clouds on the left side of the stone where there was no light or brilliancy to show the disapproval of God.

In the same way Christ is the light that is already in the heart and mind of converted souls or persons. In the wilderness sanctuary there was a means in which to get to God, but today there are no third party tools such as the altar, table of shewbread, candlesticks, or geographical boundaries such as the courtyard, holy place, or Most Holy Place. Today all of the rituals are gone, but God the Father, the Son, and the Holy Spirit are still directly acting in the converted person's life through the working of Christ in the heavenly place (1 Cor. 3:16; 6:19, 20).

With very much sadness I have to say that the problem at this junction is that most Christians are unable to demonstrate this converted Christian character. The reason being is that for a long time Christians have dwelt in the self-life, which is a very deceitful kind of lifestyle of so-called Christian garb. The Urim and Thummim provided tangible instructions from God. Our attire is made up of our own makeup, our own religious influence without instruction or direction from God.

Our belief's today are of the self-organized human maxim (cliché). All is made up to be platitudes, but they can't please God. It can't be true. The reason why the cliché can't please God is because it is self-produced. Anything with self is corrupted with selfishness. It has no self-sacrificing nature. It is conditioned by the need of the value of reciprocity. God's principle is unconditional and self-sacrificing, giving and not expecting anything in return.

When the soul (mind) is led by the Holy Spirit, the work of selfishness, which is the work of the soul or mind, is crucified (Gal. 5:24), and the believer has the mind of Christ (Phil. 2:5). Thus, the mind of Jesus, which dwells in the believer directly, causes the believer to preach the good news of redemption to all nations, kindred, tongue, tribe, and people without any partiality just as Jesus did.

The Holy Spirit-led mind has a mind like Christ and Christ alone. It teaches the truth because the Holy Spirit dwells in the believer's spirit in much the same manner as how God sat in the Most Holy Place.

This manifestation or phenomenon can happen when Christians genuinely surrender self to the leadership of the Holy Spirit. Sorrowfully, many believers depend on theological, philosophical, scientific, traditional, historical, and religious education as the spiritual work of God. No matter how much education one receives it cannot solve the problem of sin of the soul. That is the main reason today that Christendom has several hundred denominations rather than being united under Christ. The same Christ has been divided into many denominations.

Christ is not there. God is not in the center of religious strife of so-called Christianity. All of the divisions are due to the strife within Christian religions and human maxim. There is exceedingly great deception. Because of this deception and the divisions within religious Christianity, non-believers mock Christianity.

Many unbelievers ask for proof that God is a real, true, experiential, and practical God. In order to demonstrate the God of the patriarchs, prophets, and apostles, then Christians must be free from carnality and natural selfishness and self-made Christianity. Self-made Christianity never pleases God.

The great danger of carnal Christianity is that it leads to legalism or antinomianism, both of which are against God and both of which are the enemies of God and His perfect will of redemption for humanity.

Legalism produces self-righteousness. Man-made religion attempts to make up it own righteousness based on self-merit. There is no place for legalism or self-righteousness in God's sight. God organized the sanctuary system to remove legalism or self-salvation.

Legalism is equally as dangerous as antinomianism. Paul openly opposes legalism from the redemptive act of God for His people through the righteousness of Christ or the grace of God through faith or acceptance of the gift of God. "Knowing that a man is not justified by the works of the law, but by the faith of Jesus Christ, even we have believed in Jesus Christ, that we might be justified by the faith of Christ, and not by the works of the law: for by the works of the law shall no flesh be justified" (Gal. 2:16). The sanctuary ministry has always pointed to the ministry of the righteousness of Christ, not the performance of good works of a person doing their own good as the requirement of the law.

No person has ever kept the law of God other than Jesus. By nature, human beings are the enemy of the law of God. The law of God is holy and perfect, but humankind is the broken reed that can't hold water in itself because it is broken. There is no way for it to be fixed. It is unrecoverable!

Legalism is the false attempt of keeping the law of God by our own virtue, which in turn is the worst suicidal method of so-called legalists. The sanctuary service invites everybody to have hope and aspirations by coming to God without carrying baggage.

The sanctuary service is the call of God for free reconciliation for the sinner or transgressor of the law of God. Anyone who comes to God will not or cannot leave without God solving their problem of sin. Therefore, self can't redeem itself by any means. Understanding this, people need to come to God as they are.

"Come unto me, all ye that labour and are heavy laden, and I will give you rest. Take my yoke upon you, and learn of me; for I am meek and lowly in heart: and ye shall find rest unto your souls. For my yoke is easy, and my burden is light" (Matt. 11:28-30).

God's sanctuary ministry is a constant invitation for humanity to come to Him in order to obtain freedom from the bondage of the self-redemptive destruction of legalism and the deadly self-destructive act of antinomianism.

Antinomianism is against the holy and perfect law of God. Antinomianism is contrary to God, which is evident in the very word itself. In the Greek origin, "anti" means against and "nomi" is the law of God. Therefore, antinomianism is claiming to have faith in Christ but not caring for the law of God. This kind of belief is believing in cheap grace. Christ and the apostles clearly address the law and its relationship to our salvation. The very fact that Christ was crucified on the cross because of the transgression of the law of God tells us plenty. So the law of God is the immutable principle of God. But rather than change His law or the principle of it, He gave Himself in place of His law for the transgression of humanity.

There is scriptural proof that Christ is not against His own law. "Think not that I am come to destroy the law, or the prophets: I am not come to destroy, but to fulfil. For verily I say unto you, Till heaven and earth pass, one jot or one title shall in no wise pass from the law, till all be fulfilled. Whosoever therefore shall break one of these least commandments, and shall teach men so, he shall be called the least in the kingdom of heaven: but whosoever shall do and teach them, the same shall be called great in the kingdom of heaven" (Matt. 5:17-19).

This text clearly states that the law of God is holy, perfect, unbreakable, unchangeable, and eternal. With this in mind, antinomianism is truly the enmity of the truth and the principles or character of God. The apostle Paul, the hero of the righteousness of Jesus or justification by faith, confirms that antinomianism has nothing to do with the salvation of Jesus Christ. Antinomianism is either ignorantly or purposely against God and His principles. Paul addressed it in the following manner: "Wherefore the law is holy, and the commandment holy, and just, and good.... For we know that the law is spiritual: but I am carnal, sold under sin" (Rom. 7:12, 14).

If the law is holy, just, good, and spiritual, then it is the nature or essence of

God. Because God is good, holy, just, and spiritual; therefore, anyone against the law of God is under the curse and condemnation of the law. Lawbreakers are under the punishment of the law.

Again, Paul displays the truth in regards to antinomianism by saying this, "But if, while we seek to be justified by Christ, we ourselves also are found sinners, is therefore Christ the minister of sin? God forbid. For if I build again the things which I destroyed, I make myself a transgressor. For I through the law am dead to the law, that I might live unto God. I am crucified with Christ: nevertheless I live; yet not I, but Christ liveth in me: and the life which I now live in the flesh I live by the faith of the Son of God, who loved me, and gave himself for me" (Gal. 2:17-20). "Do we then make void the law through faith? God forbid: yea, we establish the law" (Rom. 3:31).

So, both the entertainment of legalism and antinomianism ceases forever in the realm of the sanctuary ministry. Both legalism and antinomianism are opposites of each other. They are both made up of a human philosophy about godliness but not truthfulness of God. So both are terms against each other and against God, too. Self only agrees with itself, no one or nothing else. The philosophy of self is always against the sanctuary ministry. The sanctuary ministry originated from God, and in and of itself it is a self-sacrificing service.

Self originates from the human soul or mind that is unconverted. An unconverted soul (mind) is always deceitful. Deception is the work of Satan who is the originator of iniquity, which causes the soul (mind) to serve only itself. Selfishness or iniquity always bends to itself only. It doesn't even know who God is. If self knows God, it is only based on fear for its wickedness and fear of punishment or judgment.

A self-sacrificing life pleases God and allows His Spirit to come and dwell in the converted Christian's life. One of the outstanding prophets of the Old Testament was Joel. He counseled the people regarding their relationship with God.

> "Therefore also now, saith the LORD, turn ye even to me with all your heart, and with fasting, and with weeping, and with mourning: And rend your heart, and not your garments, and turn unto the LORD your God: for he is gracious and merciful, slow to anger, and of great kindness, and repenteth him of the evil. Who knoweth if he will return

and repent, and leave a blessing behind him; even a meat offering and a drink offering unto the LORD your God? Blow the trumpet in Zion, sanctify a fast, call a solemn assembly: Gather the people, sanctify the congregation, assemble the elders, gather the children, and those that suck the breasts: let the bridegroom go forth of his chamber, and the bride out of her closet. Let the priests, the ministers of the LORD, weep between the porch and the altar, and let them say, Spare thy people, O LORD, and give not thine heritage to reproach, that the heathen should rule over them: wherefore should they say among the people, Where is their God?" (Joel 2:12-17).

Even today, what is needed is men and women who will stand up and call people of God from waywardness of antinomianism and legalism back to the LORD God who is merciful and always gracious, loving, kind, and compassionate.

Men and women are created and born to honor God with their spirit, soul, and body, with faithfulness, persistency, consistency, and self-sacrificing obedience. This can only be possible when converted Christians apply the cross of Christ to their lives. Christians must start enjoying or rejoicing in the suffering of Christ Jesus. What does this mean? There are two outstanding scriptural admonitions on this subject. "And if children, then heirs; heirs of God, and joint-heirs with Christ; if so be that we suffer with him, that we may be also glorified together" (Rom. 8:17). "Forasmuch then as Christ hath suffered for us in the flesh, arm yourselves likewise with the same mind: for he that hath suffered in the flesh hath ceased from sin" (1 Pet. 4:1).

Before the crown, there is always a cross to bear. Christ earned the glory, and we gained the glory. We receive the glory of God as a gift if we accept the cross of Christ by faith. Christ worked out the way for us. Ours is the victory by faith, trusting, and obeying. He, Christ, became victorious in mind/soul. His mind demanded of Him, like it does of us, that He was to fulfill the desires of the mind, but Christ always said "No!"

The reader of Romans 8:1-13 will notice that Christ condemned the law of sin or flesh in the mind. Peter, who was an eyewitness of Christ both physically and spiritually, found that Jesus Christ controlled the desires of the flesh in His own mind; because He did this, he was in perfect harmony with His Father and the Holy Spirit in spirit, soul (mind), and body.

Christ was always consistent in depending on the Spirit of God from His conception to His crucifixion. He was fully loyal to God and consistent in depending on the work of the Holy Spirit in His life. This caused Him to obey God rather than succumbing to the works of the mind/soul.

As humans, our selfish, corrupt mind is independent from God, and it often wants to do whatever is contrary to God. But it always leads people to a state of loss or destruction. But Jesus conquered self and relied fully on God. Peter also encouraged believers to conquer the works of the flesh and glorify God in the same manner as Paul who said, "I live; yet not I, but Christ liveth in me: and the life which I now live in the flesh I live by the faith of the Son of God" (Gal. 2:20).

Enoch walked with God by faith and was translated without seeing physical death (Heb. 11:5). Today's Christians may make all kinds of excuses for not glorifying God, but it is possible to walk with God.

The selfless soul is the one who pleases God and brings hope to those who are in the dark, freeing them by teaching them about God, a God of love rather than a God of tyranny. Through His followers, God is illuminating the world with the hope of Christ's soon return and the good news of redemption.

The psalmist set an example for all believers when he said, "O how love I thy law! it is my meditation all the day. Thou through thy commandments hast made me wiser than mine enemies: for they are ever with me. I have more understanding than all my teachers: for thy testimonies are my meditation. I understand more than the ancients, because I keep thy precepts. I have refrained my feet from every evil way, that I might keep thy word. I have not departed from thy judgments: for thou hast taught me. How sweet are thy words unto my taste! yea, sweeter than honey to my mouth! Through thy precepts I get understanding: therefore I hate every false way" (Ps. 119:97-105).

True believers appreciate the true principles of God and love the commandments of God. They recognize that the commandments of God are the source of life, wisdom, comfort, understanding, protection, learning, joy, and truth. Here the psalmist is speaking of the believer who was forgiven by God from the sanctuary of God. Total separation from sin caused him to fall in love with God and His commandments, just as Jesus was totally obedient and followed God's laws.

Converted persons are perfectly obedient to God and serve Him in glory and truth. Jesus alluded to this truth when speaking to His disciples in the writing of Matthew: "Be ye therefore perfect, even as your Father which is in heaven is perfect" (Matt. 5:48).

In this verse the implication is that the forgiven sinner accepts the abundance of the forgiveness of God and grows to the maturity and character development or mind/soul agreement with God. If the mind/soul fully agrees with the body, the body is in harmony with the mind/soul because the body only accomplishes what the mind/soul directs. The body is obedient to the mind/soul. The reason being for this is that the mind now is the mind of Christ being led by the Spirit of God—the one who dwells in the spirit of the converted believer. In turn, the mind of Christ controls the desires of the flesh or body because the converted believer no longer walks in the flesh but in the Spirit of God, which dwells in the spirit of the believer.

What is the work, benefits, dangers, or damages the body can do? Let's look at the body with its true nature and behavior.

Body

This is the center of expression or manifestation of the mind/soul. In here the soul is commander-in-chief of the body. Whatever the mind says or agrees with, the body fulfills, or whatever the body wants to do, the soul/mind of the unconverted believer or non-believer must consent to. They work in harmony to manifest the work of the flesh or the work of iniquity.

This is where all of the emotional desires of the human body or the mind either consent or reject something. When the mind rejects the demands of the body, then the mind suffers and the flesh suffers too. The real suffering of the mind comes from not satisfying the desires of the body, such as inappropriate appetite, eating excessively, illicit sex, false love, hate, discrimination, tribalism, nationalism, false fame, self-exaltation, self-gratification, self-righteousness, etc., that are against the will of God and serve self interests. Because of this, humanity must rely on Christ to gain victory over the flesh.

"Forasmuch then as Christ hath suffered for us in the flesh, arm yourselves likewise with the same mind: for he that hath suffered in the flesh hath ceased from sin; That he no longer should live the rest of his time in the flesh to the lusts of men, but to the will of God" (1 Pet. 4:1, 2).

The apostle Paul relates almost the same idea in Galatians: "And they that are Christ's have crucified the flesh with the affections and lusts" (Gal. 5:24).

John also warns all generations with this statement: "For all that is in the world, the lust of the flesh, and the lust of the eyes, and the pride of life, is not of the Father, but is of the world. And the world passeth away, and the lust thereof: but he that doeth the will of God abideth for ever" (1 John 2:16).

The body is sinful and carnal. The apostle Paul refers to it in this way: "Knowing this, that our old man is crucified with him, that the body of sin might be destroyed, that henceforth we should not serve sin. For he that is dead is freed from sin" (Rom. 6:6, 7).

The body of the unconverted mind serves the perverted his/her life, representing the courtyard of the wilderness sanctuary. Paul offered the following counsel to the church in Corinth: "Know ye not that ye are the temple of God, and that the Spirit of God dwelleth in you? If any man defile the temple of God, him shall God destroy; for the temple of God is holy, which temple ye are" (1 Cor. 3:16, 17).

All in all the body, which is the temple of God, represents the place where the altar of the sacrificial lamb was slain every day two times daily. The courtyard service is where every member of the congregation could see and listen to the forgiveness of sin and witness the slaying of the innocent animal on behalf of the sinner's transgression of the law of God

The courtyard was an open space of the sanctuary for the people of God. The body represents the courtyard because the physical frame of humanity is that which everyone can see directly. No one can easily see the mind/soul or spirit of a man. Even the expression of the mind/soul and spirit are only displayed through the works of the body. That's the main reason God said, "Your body is the temple of God."

The expressions of righteousness or sin are displayed in the body. The converted persons' actions are eyed as the righteousness of God because they are conducted by the Spirit of God, which dwells in the spirit of human beings and conducts the believers' mind. The fruit of the spirit will be evident in the lives of God's followers (Gal. 5:22, 23). That is the main reason the mind of the converted believer produces the fruit of the Holy Spirit. Christ also echoes this statement when He said, "I am the vine, ye are the branches: He that abideth in me, and I in him, the same bringeth forth much fruit: for without me ye can do nothing" (John 15:5).

These fruits or "much fruit" are the fruits that the converted believer can bear through the indwelling Spirit of God in the spirit and mind of man.

On the other hand, the unconverted mind produces fruits of iniquities. "Now the works of the flesh are manifest, which are these; adultery, fornication, uncleanness, lasciviousness, idolatry, witchcraft, hatred, variance, emulations, wrath, strife, seditions, heresies, envying, murders, drunkenness, revellings, and such like: of the which I tell you before, as I have also told you in time past, that they which do such things shall not inherit the kingdom of God" (Gal. 5:19-21).

These and many other vices completely defile people and destroy the path of life. These actions also separate people from the God who created them for His special purpose of glorifying Him and ruling the entire earthly creation (Gen. 1:26, 27).

When Adam and Eve sinned, they lost their glorious character and fell into the sinful trap of Satan. This problem is not only a problem for the unbeliever but it is also a problem for carnal Christians. For a long time, man-made Christianity, which originated or was organized for self-gratification or self-exaltation, has reigned on earth in the name of Christ. While people call themselves Christians, many are full of deception or self-righteousness.

In some respects, it is much easier to approach and teach and save a non-believer than a carnal Christian. Carnal Christians are very proud of their own religiosity, and they defend their own beliefs. Non-believers either accept Christ and are saved or they deny God and are lost. Carnal Christianity is polluted with the selfish act of sin. The carnal Christian does basically the same sinful practices as the non-believer does; the only difference is the level of the sinful practice. The non-believer loves sinful activities, such as the ones listed in Galatians 5:19-21, but the carnal Christian loves the self-righteous act of sin. Christ calls this hypocrisy in Matthew 23:13-15, and previously in the Old Testament He called it iniquity or wickedness and deception (Isa. 64:6; Jer. 17:9).

These types of people like to talk and do what they believe is right just for show, but it is not for God. They only play the part of being a Christian to look good or right before others. God, with His infinite wisdom, searches the heart and knows the true motive of the heart.

> "Not every one that saith unto me, Lord, Lord, shall enter into the kingdom of heaven; but he that doeth the will of my Father which is in heaven. Many will say to me in that day, Lord, Lord, have we not prophesied in thy name? and in thy name have cast out devils? and in thy name done many wonderful works? And then will I profess unto them, I never knew you: depart from me, ye that work iniquity" (Matt. 7:21-23).

The work of the flesh is extremely deceitful. It tries to imitate the truth, but it can never be true. It has no genes to the truth in the imitation. Actually, whatever flesh comes up with when measured against God's standards is iniquity. No matter how good the work of the flesh looks and tries to appear in its best and wonderful light, God will never accept it because Christ condemns it as iniquity.

Therefore, in order to please God, the believer as a whole must surrender self to the cross of Christ by faith. The cross of Christ is the best place for sinful and carnal individuals to say good-bye to self. When self is in control, God is not there. Self makes one a slave of Satan, sin, the world, and death. Following self leads one down a destructive path. God and godliness offers freedom, eternal life, redemption, and glorification. God and godliness are life and freedom.

In the same manner as a dead persons cannot please God, someone who is dead to sin cannot be *displeasing* to God. The apostle Paul wrote, "Likewise reckon ye also yourselves to be dead indeed unto sin, but alive unto God through Jesus Christ our Lord" (Rom. 6:11).

A converted Christian metamorphoses into Christ's likeness through the work of the Holy Spirit by faith. Such a person is the one who is the temple or sanctuary of God where God Himself abides for the ministration of redemption to other human beings. God's purpose all in all for His creation was, is, and will be to restore humanity for His service and glory forever.

A converted individual is a sanctuary of God and becomes the abiding place of God on earth. Once and for all, when a converted man or church body reckons its own self as dead to sin, God immediately dwells in the spirit, soul, and body and begins to manifest all the works of God in the same manner. Christ is then truly manifested on earth. In fact, Christ said, "Verily, verily, I say unto you, He that believeth on me, the works that I do shall he do also; and greater works than these shall he do; because I go unto my Father. And whatsoever ye shall ask in my name, that will I do, that the Father may be glorified in the Son. If ye shall ask any thing in my name, I will do it.... Even the Spirit of truth; whom the world cannot receive, because it seeth him not, neither knoweth him: but ye know him; for he dwelleth with you, and shall be in you" (John 14:12-17).

This is the main reason that Joseph, Daniel, Esther, Ruth, Mary Magdalene, and so many other biblical heroes were able to glorify God the Father with a noble character and godliness. The Holy Spirit was dwelling in their soul. These men and women suffered for Jesus Christ and experienced difficult situations throughout their lives (1 Pet. 4:1). But they defeated the work or desires of the sinful flesh in full, and they became victorious over the work of Satan.

When God dwells in the life of the believer, he/she takes on the heritage of the Father, Son, and Holy Spirit. This is definitely the sanctuary. Genuinely converted souls are ones who enlighten the whole world with the goodness of the gospel of Jesus Christ as He commissioned His disciples and all believers to do so. "Ye are the light of the world. A city that is set on an hill cannot be hid. Neither do men light a candle, and put it under a bushel, but on a candlestick; and it giveth light unto all that are in the house" (Matt. 5:14, 15).

The sanctuary did not have any windows, but there had to be a light shining within it night and day without interruption. This ceaseless light flowed directly from God Himself who dwelt in the Most Holy Place. God is light and life to all creation, which was manifested through the sanctuary ministry. This is the same God who said, "Ye are the light of the world," meaning those who are genuine believers who have accepted the sanctuary ministry of God. In human beings the three compartments represent the Most Holy Place, which is the spirit, the holy place, which is the soul, and the body, which is the courtyard.

Without controversy, humankind is the temple of God on earth (1 Cor. 3:16; 6:19, 20; 2 Cor. 6:16). To make it clear that converted believers are the sanctuary of God on earth, let us look at some scriptural specifications in the following texts.

Body as the Courtyard

"I beseech you therefore, brethren, by the mercies of God, that ye present your bodies a living sacrifice, holy, acceptable unto God, which is your reasonable service.... So we, being many, are one body in Christ, and every one members one of another" (Rom. 12:1, 5).

This section of the text explains that the *body* is the *courtyard*. Christ gave His own life for public display to suffer like the sacrificial lamb to redeem all humankind who believe in Him and to completely remove sin from the universe of God one day soon.

Soul as the Holy Place

"For who hath known the mind of the Lord, that he may instruct him? But we have the mind of Christ" (1 Cor. 2:16).

As previously established the mind/soul of man represents the holy place or the place of daily ministry. For sure the mind/soul is the center of every activity of humankind, whether the person believes in God or not. Therefore, as the holy place was the center of the daily services for the forgiveness of sin, so also the mind/soul of the converted believer is the center of the work of God and the message of hope and grace of Jesus, the love of the Father, and the fellowship of the Holy Ghost.

The converted mind is the center of communication or the center of the nervous system of the spirit and body. Converted Christians are those who receive order from the Spirit of God, which resides and operates in the converted believers' spirit and directs and guides the mind and body to be obedient to righteousness (justification), holiness (sanctification), wisdom, and glorification of God. The converted soul is the very essence of God's glory in His daily activities. Christians such as Enoch, Joseph, Ruth, Esther, Job, Daniel, John the Baptist, Stephen, Paul, and John the Revelator glorified

God. There have been millions of people throughout earth's history who have manifested the character of God on earth.

Such converted characters God calls "born of God" and the partakers of the divine nature of God. Paul also repeatedly admonishes Christians to have the mind and body of Christ so that the soul and body may be filled with the fullness of the Spirit of God (Rom. 12:2; 1 Cor. 2:16; Phil. 2:5).

Through the work of the Holy Spirit in the spirit of each individual, the converted Christian is the abiding place of God in His fullness (sanctuary of God) where the ministry of reconciliation or the atonement of God takes place in the believer's life. This ministry of reconciliation or atonement has been given to believers so that they will function as representatives on this earth to enhance the work of God for the second advent of Christ.

The apostle Paul certifies that God Himself by His own will has given the converted believer the ministry of atonement to serve as His representative or ambassador. "And all things are of God, who hath reconciled us to himself by Jesus Christ, and hath given to us the ministry of reconciliation; To wit, that God was in Christ, reconciling the world unto himself, not imputing their trespasses unto them; and hath committed unto us the word of reconciliation. Now then we are ambassadors for Christ, as though God did beseech you by us: we pray you in Christ's stead, be ye reconciled to God" (2 Cor. 5:18-20).

When Jesus was on earth, He instructed His disciples and all future generation to share the message of His love with the world. As His followers, Jesus has named us His heirs, royalty, and ambassadors (Rev. 1:6; Rom. 8:17; John 15:4, 5; Zech. 2:8; Isa. 49:16; 2 Cor. 5:20).

Spirit as the Most Holy Place

"The Spirit itself beareth witness with our spirit, that we are the children of God" (Rom. 8:16). This message is very clear—the Holy Spirit dwells in the spirit of the converted believer. The children of God are obedient to all of God's laws, but the children of the devil commit sin (1 John 3:8).

The converted believer becomes the earthly sanctuary or the temple of God. God through Christ sanctifies the whole person (John 17:17). Jesus Christ redeems humanity by paying the wages of sin and restoring the unity between

God and people and the unity between one another. There is no Greek/Gentile, no Jew, no man, no woman in the gospel of Jesus Christ; all are one and the same. During this process, the Sanctifier and the sanctified believer become one. The whole purpose of the Sanctifier's crucifixion was the ministry of atonement and the restoration of a relationship between God and humanity. Jesus made the following statements:

> "That they all may be one; as thou, Father, art in me, and I in thee, that they also may be one in us: that the world may believe that thou hast sent me. And the glory which thou gavest me I have given them; that they may be one, even as we are one: I in them, and thou in me, that they may be made perfect in one; and that the world may know that thou hast sent me, and hast loved them, as thou hast loved me" (John 17:21-23).

> "Wherefore I say unto you, All manner of sin and blasphemy shall be forgiven unto men: but the blasphemy against the Holy Ghost shall not be forgiven unto men. And whosoever speaketh a word against the Son of man, it shall be forgiven him: but whosoever speaketh against the Holy Ghost, it shall not be forgiven him, neither in this world, neither in the world to come" (Matt. 12:32, 33).

In these texts, Christ is referring to the indwelling of the Holy Spirit, which is God—"God is a Spirit" (John 4:24). Therefore, those who allow the Holy Spirit to dwell in them are the sanctuary of God (2 Cor. 6:16; 1 Cor. 3:16; 6:19, 20).

As the sanctuary of God, the believer will reflect the changes God is making in his/her life. Paul addresses some of these changes and the importance of hiding God's laws in our heart (2 Corinthians 3:1-18). God wrote his character and instructions on two tables of stone and preserved them in the tabernacle of God in the Most Holy Place.

When the law of God demands justice for the transgressor of God's law, then the mercy of God steps in and God forgives His people. That same process was in place in the wilderness sanctuary with the ministration of the priests of God. When the ministration of the atonement was done, God's great glory was manifested in the sanctuary on that very day. The sanctuary system was established on the day that the sanctuary was completed (Exod. 40:34-38).

God commanded Moses to put the Ten Commandments into the ark of the covenant. It was in the tabernacle that the Shekinah glory was manifested in the wilderness with the Israelites and that same glory shines forth from genuine believers (1 Cor. 6:19, 20). God ordered Christ to write His commandments in the heart of humankind so that Christians and the church would carry the same Shekinah glory of God with them. Paul repeatedly clarifies that human beings are exceedingly greater and more glorious than the wooden temple in the wilderness. If the ministration of the wooden wilderness tabernacle was that glorious and the Shekinah glory or the very presence of God was there, then how much more is the temple of humanity.

God is more glorious in the human spirit, soul, and body, which has been sanctified by the blood of the eternal Godhead, Jesus Christ, and the indwelling of God. Human beings are the true habitation of God because we share the true life of God in "image and likeness" and are partakers of the divine nature of God (Gen. 1:26; 2:7; 2 Pet. 1:4). Therefore, humankind is the true habitation of God. These texts certainly verify that converted believers or Christians or the church body are the sanctuary of God. Let's take a look at them and analyze them very carefully.

> "And God said, Let us make man in our image, after our likeness: and let them have dominion over the fish of the sea, and over the fowl of the air, and over the cattle, and over all the earth, and over every creeping thing that creepeth upon the earth" (Gen. 1:26).

> "And the LORD God formed man of the dust of the ground, and breathed into his nostrils the breath of life; and man became a living soul" (Gen. 2:7).

> "In whom all the building fitly framed together groweth unto an holy temple in the Lord: In whom ye also are builded together for an habitation of God through the Spirit" (Eph. 2:21, 22).

> "Whereby are given unto us exceeding great and precious promises: that by these ye might be partakers of the divine nature, having es-

caped the corruption that is in the world through lust" (2 Pet. 1:4).

The converted person is certainly the abiding place of God. Therefore, the sanctuary was the abiding place of God, so also is the converted person's spirit, soul, and body the temple of God. God sent the disciples to spread the gospel throughout the world as the commissioners of the ministers of reconciliation in the Great Commission. "Go ye therefore, and teach all nations, baptizing them in the name of the Father, and of the Son, and of the Holy Ghost" (Matt. 28:19).

Paul also states that, "And all things are of God, who hath reconciled us to himself by Jesus Christ, and hath given to us the ministry of reconciliation; To wit, that God was in Christ, reconciling the world unto himself, not imputing their trespasses unto them; and hath committed unto us the word of reconciliation. Now then we are ambassadors for Christ, as though God did beseech you by us: we pray you in Christ's stead, be ye reconciled to God" (2 Cor. 5:18-20).

God has given this last generation as the ministers of reconciliation in the same manner as the priests served in the wilderness sanctuary by offering the blood of innocent animals. Today's believers are the ministers for our generation through the blood of innocent Lamb, Christ Jesus, dwelling in the temple of our body, soul, and spirit (1 Thess. 5:23). As Christ's ministers, it is our duty to share the message of His love with the world.

Chapter 5

God's Work in the Heavenly Sanctuary

Revelation of the Sanctuary Ministry to the Remnant Church

When God sent His Son to be incarnated into human flesh and blood to redeem or restore human beings to their original status, the generation failed itself and failed God in understanding what He was doing. Humanity rejected the ministry of Christ and then killed Him.

The Divine took sinful humanity on Himself and shared the divinity of God with humankind. The incarnation was the reconciliation of God with His creation. But the people couldn't see the truth and couldn't understand what God had planned, so they became the archenemy of God and mercilessly, ruthlessly crucified Christ. Sinful and selfish individuals united with Satan against Christ to break down the atonement. The sanctuary ministry, which has always been God's mercy, righteousness, sanctification, wisdom, and redemption, was objected and opposed too.

The sanctuary ministry is the righteousness of God because God didn't give up on humankind. Even the people who were reading the Scriptures didn't really and fully understand what the atonement ministry was from the time of John the Revelator until God Himself revealed the true view of the glorious sanctuary message, which is the righteousness of God (justification and sanctification), to the Seventh-day Adventist leaders between 1844 and 1846 after the Great Disappointment on October 22, 1844. Many Christians today have missed the understanding of the Great Disappointment of October 22, 1844, and the relationship of the Seventh-day Adventist Church.

This kind of misunderstanding led many Christians to misunderstand the Seventh-day Adventist Christian message. Let the record show that the Seventh-day Adventist Church was organized in 1846, two years after the Great Disappointment. The failing or disappointment occurred based on the misunderstanding of non-Seventh-day Adventist Christians who felt that the cleansing of the sanctuary of Daniel 8:14 or 2300 days was the second coming of Jesus Christ to clean this earth with fire. Because the talk was about the cleansing of the sanctuary, they felt and interpreted the sanctuary as the earth, not the heavenly sanctuary.

Though they had calculated the right dates for the cleansing of the sanctuary, they had failed to understand the truth of the cleansing of the heavenly sanctuary. The Protestant Christians thought that the cleansing of the sanctuary was the cleansing of the earth by fire at the second coming of Christ.

Many accepted this view to the point that the Great Disappointment devastated thousands of families in America and Europe who resigned themselves to the fact that their long-awaited Redeemer was not coming.

Weeks and months later after much intense study of the sanctuary God revealed to His disappointed servants that the cleansing that was to be done was not the second advent of Christ but rather the beginning of the work of Christ in the Most Holy Place in the heavenly sanctuary, interceding for all believers who genuinely accept Christ Jesus as their personal Savior.

Some of the offspring of those who were disappointed were given light to discover this blessed hope. Their hearts thrilled with the revelation, and they started studying the truth like the people of Berea (Acts 17:10, 11). God slowly revealed more insight and prophecy as they studied, until the present truth of the sanctuary's cleansing and a true biblical view of the heavenly sanctuary were understood.

The small group of believers continued to study and teach the new insight of the true understanding of the sanctuary in New England and wherever else they were invited to speak.

The result of these studies and the believers who preached the truth was the formation of the Seventh-day Adventist Church. The church was founded on an understanding of Bible prophecy and the commandments of God.

The new insights at that time began with the historical prophecy of the decree of Artaxerxes, the emperor of Persia in 457 BC. Artaxerxes granted Ezra permission to re-build the temple (Ezra 7:1-26). Based on the prophecy of Daniel 8:14 and the 2300 days and Daniel 9:23-27, and the 70 weeks, the time began in 457 BC and ended on AD 34 and 62 weeks (Dan. 9:26), which is 7 weeks from 457 BC and the building of Jerusalem and the restoration of the sanctuary or 49 years, at which time the city and temple were restored or completed in the fall of 408 BC, Sixty-two weeks from the restoration of the city and temple (408 BC–27 AD) Christ was baptized and started His public ministry. In AD 31 the Messiah was cutoff or crucified, and at the end of that one week, Jesus was rejected which was the true or main atonement and the last atonement ministry of earth, which is the gospel of good news and glad tidings of God.

The sanctuary story summarized in Daniel 9:23-27 is very crucial in understanding what is related to the redemption of the restoration of Jerusalem and the temple from the Babylonian captivity for the date of 457 BC and Christ physically proclaiming that the kingdom of God and humanity no longer belong to the enemy, Satan. There are those who are not the property of Satan but belong to God and glorify the body of Christ. The freedom of humankind was established through the covenant relationship of the atonement of Christ on the cross.

Redemption and freedom from the bondage of the enemy was completed through Christ's earthly ministry and atoning death on the cross (Luke 4:16-19). Through the ages teachings and Old Testament prophecy have centered on this theme. In 1844 at the end of the 2300 days, Christ entered the sanctuary and began judging the world and atoning believers who have accepted Christ's free gift of salvation (Dan. 7:9, 13).

After Christ's crucifixion and resurrection, He ascended to the heavenly sanctuary and entered the holy place, where He finished the work of the daily ministry in the same manner as the earthy sanctuary ministry until 1844.

To understand the 2300 days prophecy, please see the following diagram:

Christians persisted in studying the Scriptures in spite of the darkest moments of the Great Disappointment. Shortly thereafter, the Adventist Church was organized, and its founding members continued to study the

Scriptures and uncover new truths. The Adventist not only discovered the true understanding of the 2300 day prophecy but they also discovered the 1260 day or 42 month prophecy that started in AD 538 until AD 1798, which was the era of papal supremacy in Europe over all Christians and political powers. The diagram on page 95 also contains information about this time period.

The Seventh-day Adventists not only grasped the 2300- and 1260-day prophetic principles but they also had biblical truth to substantiate what they were saying. If you do not believe this, then please read the fundamental beliefs of the Seventh-day Adventist Church.

If Seventh-day Adventists are accurate in historical and biblical doctrines, do the members of this remnant church still need the sanctuary message today? Yes, all the members need it afresh now more than ever. The sanctuary ministry is not a doctrine; rather, it is the very presence of God or indwelling of God in the believers' life in the same manner as God was in the Most Holy Place among the people in the wilderness sanctuary.

Seventh-day Adventists didn't uncover the sanctuary truth by their genuine study of the Scriptures only; God revealed the sanctuary ministry and many important biblical truths through Ellen G. White, a prophet of God whose teachings are in harmony with the Bible and whose counsel was often way before her time.

God elected her for this last generation to augment the three angels' messages and the teaching of the righteousness of Christ for all the human race so as many people as possible may be freed from the bondage of Satan through knowledge of the truth (Rev. 14:6-12).

The sanctuary message is the message of the righteousness of God and the atonement of humanity through Jesus' sacrifice. It is the message of God's reconciliation with humankind. The sanctuary message points to Jesus' righteousness who put Himself in jeopardy of the second death on behalf of humankind by taking on the sins of the world at the cross.

He died in the place of all who have sinned, freeing everyone who believes in Him as their personal Savior (John 3:16). The very existence of the movement or message of the Seventh-day Adventist Church is to preach and teach the sanctuary message. This message is the healing balm for sin-suffered humanity.

2300 Days (Years)
Prophecy Made Simple
With the Principle of Day-Year
Ezekiel 4:6 & Numbers 14:34

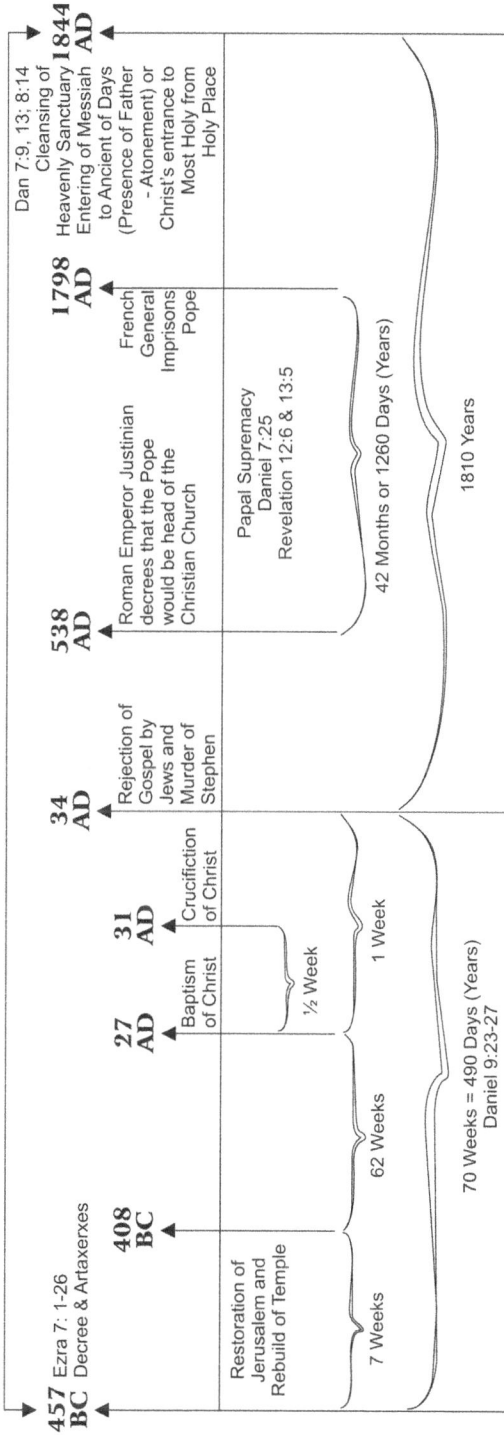

457 BC — Ezra 7: 1-26 Decree & Artaxerxes

408 BC

Restoration of Jerusalem and Rebuild of Temple

7 Weeks

27 AD — Baptism of Christ

31 AD — Crucifiction of Christ

½ Week

1 Week

62 Weeks

70 Weeks = 490 Days (Years)
Daniel 9:23-27

34 AD — Rejection of Gospel by Jews and Murder of Stephen

538 AD — Roman Emperor Justinian decrees that the Pope would be head of the Christian Church

Papal Supremacy
Daniel 7:25
Revelation 12:6 & 13:5

42 Months or 1260 Days (Years)

1798 AD — French General Imprisons Pope

1810 Years

1844 AD — Dan 7:9, 13; 8:14 Cleansing of Heavenly Sanctuary Entering of Messiah to Ancient of Days (Presence of Father - Atonement) or Christ's entrance to Most Holy from Holy Place

Fig.2

95

As we established before, the sanctuary ministry is God's loving service to humanity so that the whole human race may understand the work of atonement and its importance. Christ became Emmanuel and died on the cross at which time the wooden sanctuary was no longer needed. He then established the new sanctuary within humanity that those who believe may genuinely become the sanctuary of God (1 Cor. 3:16; 6:19, 20; 2 Pet. 1:4; Gal. 2:20; Eph. 3:19; 2 Cor. 6:16; Eph. 1:22, 23; 2:18-22).

God's whole goal is to restore humanity to the relationship He enjoyed with them before the fall. He seeks to dwell with us here on earth and prepare us for heaven. Read the following texts that Paul wrote concerning God's desires. "And what agreement hath the temple of God with idols? for ye are the temple of the living God; as God hath said, I will dwell in them, and walk in them; and I will be their God, and they shall be my people" (2 Cor. 6:16). "In whom all the building fitly framed together groweth unto an holy temple in the Lord: In whom ye also are builded together for an habitation of God through the Spirit" (Eph. 2:21, 22).

King David understood God's desire to have a relationship with His children. In Psalm 139:8-12 he contemplates the omnipresence of God: "If I ascend up into heaven, thou art there: if I make my bed in hell, behold, thou art there. If I take the wings of the morning, and dwell in the uttermost parts of the sea; Even there shall thy hand lead me, and thy right hand shall hold me. If I say, Surely the darkness shall cover me; even the night shall be light about me. Yea, the darkness hideth not from thee; but the night shineth as the day: the darkness and the light are both alike to thee."

Just as God desired to be with the Israelites in the wilderness and therefore dwelt in the sanctuary, so he desires to be with His children today through the indwelling of the Holy Spirit. And as His disciple, He has commissions all those who follow Him to share this good news with the world and enlighten all the nations through the three angels' messages.

"And I saw another angel fly in the midst of heaven, having the ever-lasting gospel to preach unto them that dwell on the earth, and to every nation, and kindred, and tongue, and people, Saying with a loud voice, Fear God, and give glory to him; for the hour of his judgment is come: and worship him that made heaven, and earth, and the sea, and the fountains of waters. And there followed another angel, saying, Babylon is fallen, is fallen, that great city, because she made all nations drink of the wine of the wrath of her fornication. And the third angel followed them, saying with a loud voice, If any man worship the beast and his image, and receive his mark in his forehead, or in his hand, The same shall drink of the wine of the wrath of God, which is poured out without mixture into the cup of his indignation; and he shall be tormented with fire and brimstone in the presence of the holy angels, and in the presence of the Lamb: And the smoke of their torment ascendeth up for ever and ever: and they have no rest day nor night, who worship the beast and his image, and whosoever receiveth the mark of his name. Here is the patience of the saints: here are they that keep the commandments of God, and the faith of Jesus. And I heard a voice from heaven saying unto me, Write, Blessed are the dead which die in the Lord from henceforth: Yea, saith the Spirit, that they may rest from their labours; and their works do follow them" (Rev. 14:6-13).

My question for you is this, is the three angels' messages the message of the sanctuary? YES!! God has repeatedly impressed me that all of the biblical messages are enveloped in the sanctuary services. Within the above passage, the three angels declared the gospel of reconciliation (verses 6, 7), the message of the awareness of sin (verse 8), and the message of warning in regards to the consequences of sin (verses 9-11). Finally, the passage ends with the admonition to remain strong and resist the beast and the assurance that those who do so will receive their just reward (verses 12, 13). Certainly these messages are declared and ordained by Jesus from the sanctuary where He is interceding for all who are genuine believers in His redeeming act.

It is the responsibility of God's followers to prepare the world for His return. The message must be shared with all nations, kindred, tongues, and people regardless of race, gender, religion, creed, intellect, fame, education, and status, etc.

The Heavenly Sanctuary Before Christ's Second Advent

It is very clear that the Scriptures speak about the existence of the heavenly sanctuary. Seventh-day Adventists did not formalize the sanctuary message, but its message is the scriptural foundation the Adventists built on

(Dan. 7:9, 13; 8:14; 9:23-27; Heb. 8:1, 2; 10:1-18; Rev. 4:5; 8:3; 11:19). Based on scriptural evidence, these fact are what God revealed to the early pioneers of the Seventh-day Adventist Church so that they could accurately tell the last generation about this good news before His glorious appearing in the clouds of heaven.

Before Jesus returns to this earth, He has to complete His work of reconciliation, which was performed on the cross when He gave His own life as the sacrificial Lamb. Please carefully listen and read the next paragraphs.

Let's examine the old covenant in the wilderness sanctuary. When the sacrificial goat was offered that was not the end of atonement. The high priest did not just jump out to the congregation and tell them to go home because there was no need for them to wait in the courtyard or around the sanctuary. The high priest didn't do that because the procedure had only started with the sacrificial goat. The blood of the goat after it was slain was carried by the high priest to the Most Holy Place from the courtyard where it had been killed for the sins that the people had committed throughout the year.

The high priest went through the holy place where the sin was deposited throughout the year when the priests transferred the sinners' sins onto themselves by eating the flesh of the sacrificed animal or carried the blood from the courtyard to the holy place and sprinkled it on the temple vessels. All the transgressors' sins were transferred to the priests and the temple itself. Therefore, on the Day of Atonement, the high priest carried the sins of the congregation, including his own sins, through the blood of the sacrificial goat into the Most Holy Place and the very presence of the God who revealed Himself through the Shekinah glory.

By faith God cleansed the high priest, the temple, and the congregation who were waiting outside with heart-searching prayer, confession, and deep repentance. Then God's mercy and justice came together and pardoned their sins. The high priest then came out from the temple and declared the forgiveness of God to the congregation. Finally, after a fitted person was selected from among the congregation, he escorted the scapegoat far away from the camp into the wilderness where the goat would never come back again, symbolizing that the sins of the high priest, temple, and congregation were separated from the people of God.

Even the person who escorted the scapegoat couldn't come back to the congregation without being cleansed for seven days in isolation from family, community, and all activities. This reminded the people about the seriousness of sin and the need for cleansing from evil.

The same service or atonement ministry is taking place in the heavenly sanctuary. It began when Christ died on the cross and ascended to the heavenly sanctuary. When Christ entered the heavenly sanctuary, He went to the holy place because the courtyard ceremony had been completed on this earth when Christ died on the cross, serving as the sacrificial Lamb and carrier of the sins of the world, thus forever ceasing the need for earthly sacrifices (John 3:16, 17; 19:30).

Upon His ascension Jesus began the work of intercession in the holy place, and Jesus continued until 1844 when He entered the Most Holy Place (Dan. 7:9, 13; 9:23-27). Following is insight that Paul wrote concerning the heavenly sanctuary: "Now of the things which we have spoken this is the sum: We have such an high priest, who is set on the right hand of the throne of the Majesty in the heavens; A minister of the sanctuary, and of the true tabernacle, which the Lord pitched, and not man" (Heb. 8:1, 2).

The apostle Paul clearly wrote that Christ is at the right hand of the throne of God, serving as High Priest of the heavenly sanctuary in the presence of God. Jesus is the Intercessor and High Priest who became human yet was raised from the dead and was restored to His divine nature, which He wants to impart to all those who believe in Him (Heb. 7:25-26; 2 Pet. 1:4). Paul talks extensively about Christ's sacrifice and role in heaven in Hebrews 9:11-15 and 10:12-27.

Another witness of the heavenly sanctuary was John, the beloved of Christ, who was also known as John the Revelator. Let us read the scriptural testimonies of John the Revelator:

"And out of the throne proceeded lightenings and thunderings and voices: and there were seven lamps of fire burning before the throne, which are the seven Spirits of God" (Rev. 4:5).

"And another angel came and stood at the altar, having a golden censer; and there was given unto him much incense, that he should offer it with the prayers of all saints upon the golden altar which was before the throne" (Rev. 8:3).

"And the temple of God was opened in heaven, and there was seen in his temple the ark of his testament: and there were lightnings, and voices, and thunderings, and an earthquake, and great hail" (Rev. 11:19).

The apostle John was the disciple of Christ in his younger years (Matt. 4:21), and he continued to serve Christ into his senior years, writing the book of Revelation in his old age (Rev. 1:1, 4, 9; 21:2; 22:8). John saw the vessels in the heavenly temple before the throne of God. John, in Revelation 4:5, saw seven lamps; in Revelation 8:3 he saw the golden altar, censor, and much incense; then in Revelation 11:19 he saw the "ark of his testament" in the temple of God in heaven.

Those who prudently study the Bible do not argument about the existence of the heavenly sanctuary. The truth of the sanctuary ministry is revealed in the Bible and was also brought to light through several visions that Ellen White had during her ministry.

Based on the Bible and Ellen White's writings, we know that Jesus entered the Most Holy Place in 1844 to plead for forgiveness for all transgressors before God. Jesus will continue serving in this role until the Father signals that the time has come for Jesus to return to this earth and bring His followers home to heaven. The process of the Most Holy Place is important in the atonement ministry because it is still going on today.

When Christ closes the ministry of the heavenly sanctuary, the scapegoat, Satan who is the great deceiver, will carry the full responsibility of all sin, which began in his heart, and will drink the full cup of his own iniquity with his evil spirits who associated with him by their own free will. Also, all humanity who, of their own free will, joined Satan by rejecting true doctrine, reproof, correction, and instruction of the righteousness of Christ by faith in the sanctuary ministry will drink the cup of the wrath of God because of refusing the very righteousness of Christ or God. The sanctuary ministry is the wisdom and righteousness of God; justification is all about what God did and does for the salvation of humanity, and sanctification is all about what God did and does on behalf of the believer's life to fit for the kingdom of God and redemption and the glorification of God.

If anyone rejects this privilege, it is nobody's fault but their own personal choice to be lost. God is still calling all humanity, urging everyone to repent and accept the atonement ministry in the heavenly sanctuary. When the call ends, probation will be closed in heaven. Satan will be fully responsible for the destruction of the old heaven and old earth, or for the cleansing away from the face of the Son of God (Rev. 20:11-14). Heaven and new earth will be established for God and His redeemed, and Satan and sin will be eternally destroyed. There will be no trace of iniquity or its nature to enter into heaven and the new earth.

After Christ gathers the righteous and destroys the wicked, will there be any sanctuary ministry in heaven? This question is very crucial to understand. With the guidance of the Holy Spirit and the Bible, let us discover the answer to this question.

The Heavenly Sanctuary After Christ's Second Advent

The sanctuary ministry is very important; it is an everlasting covenant relationship between God and His people. Certainly, the structural heavenly sanctuary service will end at the close of probation when Christ sends an angel from heaven saying, "He that is unjust, let him be unjust still: and he which is filthy, let him be filthy still: and he that is righteous, let him be righteous still: and he that is holy, let him be holy still. And, behold, I come quickly; and my reward is with me, to give every man according as his work shall be. I am Alpha and Omega, the beginning and the end, the first and the last" (Rev. 22:11-13).

After this statement the sanctuary ministry as a geographical structure will not exist. The reason being is that the structural principle or design was created because of the separation of humanity from God (Isa. 59:2-3). After the second advent of Christ, there will be no iniquity in heaven to separate humankind and God. Nothing will disband God from His creation. The sanctuary will be God Himself. It is written: "And I saw no temple therein: for the Lord God

Almighty and the Lamb are the temple of it" (Rev. 21:22).

This is the truth of the matter. There is no structural sanctuary or temple services or ministry in heaven after Christ's second coming, and the reason being is that no sin can enter into the presence of God (Rev. 21:27). However, Revelation 21:22 is very clear that "the LORD God Almighty and the Lamb are the temple of it [heaven]." This means there will be a temple that will be even better than the best temple ever known or written about. The reason is that God the Father, Son, and Holy Ghost become the center of worship rather than ministry.

Paul states it in a very clear manner: "Let this mind be in you, which was also in Christ Jesus: Who, being in the form of God, thought it not robbery to be equal with God: But made himself of no reputation, and took upon him the form of a servant, and was made in the likeness of men: And being found in fashion as a man, he humbled himself, and became obedient unto death, even the death of the cross" (Phil. 2:5-8).

Christ, the sacrificial Lamb, was slain in the courtyard that the blood of the sacrificial animal would be the remission of sin for the transgressors. In the same manner Jesus was crucified on the cross in public as the one who is cursed because of His own sin while He never sinned. Jesus became a curse for those who believed in Him as their hope of glory. "Christ hath redeemed us from the curse of the law, being made a curse for us: for it is written, Cursed is every one that hangeth on a tree" (Gal. 3:13).

Truly sin is a curse. Christ became that curse for the whole world and all believers. Christ was not ashamed to pay the demand of the law of God, which is the wrath of God. Because Christ made such a huge sacrifice, God the Father and the Holy Spirit have exalted Christ above all else: "Far above all principality, and power, and might, and dominion, and every name that is named, not only in this world, but also in that which is to come: And hath put all things under his feet, and gave him to be the head over all things to the church" (Eph. 1:21, 22).

Again, John the apostle amplifies that Christ was the courtyard sacrifice in different wording "For God so loved the world, that he gave his only begotten Son, that whosoever believeth in him should not perish, but have everlasting life. For God sent not his Son into the world to condemn the world; but that the world through him might be saved" (John 3:16, 17).

The whole world, if it believed in Him and in His ample provision, would be free from the bondage of Satan, sin, and death. This ample provision of His own life makes Him and His Father and the Holy Spirit worthy of worship by His redeemed and the host of holy angels. If Christ represents the courtyard sacrifice, then who represents the holy place? The Holy Spirit does.

As the daily services took place twice a day in the holy place for the forgiveness of sins, so the Holy Spirit facilitates the work of salvation through Christ and love of the Father in this world through intercessory prayer (Rom 8:26). The Holy Spirit is the true representative of the holy place because it is the center of mediation or intercession. As the priests served in the holy place and prayed for the people, it was the Holy Spirit who drew near and inspired the priest.

The scripture was written by the inspiration of the Holy Spirit (2 Pet. 1:19-21). "For the prophecy came not in old time by the will of men: but holy men of God spake as they were moved by the Holy Ghost" (verse 21). What is the connection between the writing of the Scripture and the holy place in the sanctuary? The connection is that the Scripture, which clearly details the sanctuary ministry and all prophecy, was inspired by the Holy Spirit to be accurate and true.

The Holy Spirit is ever interceding and helping do what humans cannot. "Likewise the Spirit also helpeth our infirmities: for we know not what we should pray for as we ought: but the Spirit itself maketh intercession for us with groanings which cannot be uttered. And he that searcheth the hearts knoweth what is the mind of the Spirit, because he maketh intercession for the saints according to the will of God. And we know that all things work together for good to them that love God, to them who are the called according to his purpose" (Rom. 8:26-28).

The work of intercession is part of the work of the Holy Spirit in the holy place ministry. So He personally represents the holy place ministry as Christ was the representative of the courtyard with His sacrificial death on the cross of Calvary.

The soul/mind of the believer and the Holy Spirit represent the holy place, and Christ, who represents the body of the converted follower, represents the courtyard. If Christ represents the courtyard, and the Holy Spirit represents the holy place, then the Father represents the Most Holy Place, which is also represented by the spirit of the believer.

"For ye have not received the spirit of bondage again to fear; but ye have received the Spirit of adoption, whereby we cry, Abba, Father. The Spirit itself beareth witness with our spirit, that we are the children of God" (Rom. 8:15, 16). God Himself works in our spirit to guide us into truth and holiness. God and His followers are one.

This is the process of the sanctuary ministry both on earth and in heaven. All in all the end process of the sanctuary both on earth and in heaven is to unite God and His redeemed without any noted boundaries. That is the main reason that after Christ completes the heavenly sanctuary ministry the door of probation will be closed. No more sanctuary services will be held in heaven after the second advent of Christ. After Christ returns, there will be no need for the sanctuary service because Satan and sin will be no more. God's people will worship God freely without restriction or fear.

At last the people of God will be home. "For this corruptible must put on incorruption, and this mortal must put on immortality. So when this corruptible shall have put on incorruption, and this mortal shall have put on immortality, then shall be brought to pass the saying that is written, Death is swallowed up in victory. O death, where is thy sting? O grave, where is thy victory? The sting of death is sin; and the strength of sin is the law. But thanks be to God, which giveth us the victory through our Lord Jesus Christ" (1 Cor. 15:53-57).

"And there shall be no more curse: but the throne of God and of the Lamb shall be in it; and his servants shall serve him: And they shall see his face; and his name shall be in their foreheads. And there shall be no night there; and they need no candle, neither light of the sun; for the Lord God giveth them light: and they shall reign for ever and ever" (Rev. 22:3-5).

The same unity or inseparable unity of the Father, Son, and Holy Spirit will bind the redeemed and the Redeemer. When God created humankind in His own image and likeness, He sought a close relationship with His creation (Gen. 1:26, 27). However, because of sin, humanity was separated from God until Christ redeemed His followers (John 17:21-23).

All Christians must take seriously their commission to spread the Word of

God to this last generation. Urgency is emphasized to utter to every kindred, nation, tongue, and people the eternal love, peace, and joy that comes from following Christ. Everyone can experience the indwelling of the Holy Spirit and be prepared for Christ's second coming if they will but embrace the message of redemption through the sanctuary (Rev. 21:3, 19, 22; 22:17).

The message of the sanctuary is physically shown in the following table:

Interrelated Infrastructure of the Sanctuary of God

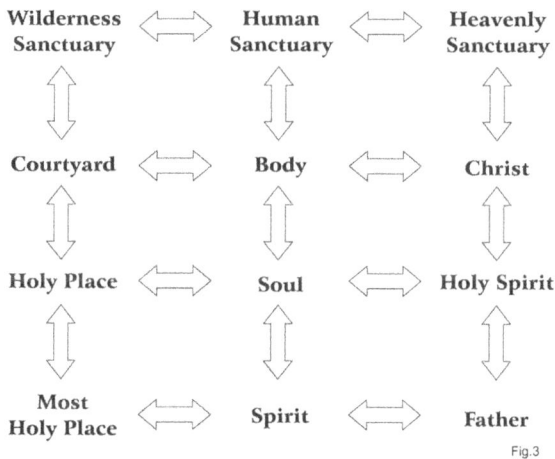

Wilderness Sanctuary	Human Sanctuary	Heavenly Sanctuary
Courtyard	Body	Christ
Holy Place	Soul	Holy Spirit
Most Holy Place	Spirit	Father

Fig.3

This diagram shows the interrelationship of God and His people. The interrelationship is called the "at-one-ment" of God and His people.

From the Beginning to the End

The sanctuary ministry can't be concluded without relating how the sanctuary ministry changed from the beginning to the present era. In the first place, in conclusion, God reminds humanity that the sanctuary is the abiding place or indwelling of God with or in His people. The abortion of the sanctuary concept started right after the fall of Adam and Eve into sin. Sin separated God and Adam and Eve and all of their descendents.

105

"But your iniquities have separated between you and your God, and your sins have hid his face from you, that he will not hear" (Isa. 59:2). "And they heard the voice of the LORD God walking in the garden in the cool of the day: and Adam and his wife hid themselves from the presence of the LORD God amongst the trees of the garden" (Gen. 3:8).

That was not the end of the story of the sanctuary ministry or the relationship of God. God again reestablished His relationship with Noah through the sign of the rainbow, which served as a promise that God wouldn't destroy the earth again (Gen. 9:13-15). But the children of Noah didn't keep a close relationship with God and didn't seek His salvation rather they sought their own. They attempted to build the Tower of Babel toward the sky to protect themselves from another flood even though God had already made a covenant with Noah that He wouldn't destroy the world again.

The children of Noah built the Tower of Babel in spite of the covenant of God. Noah's descendents failed to follow the holy and true instruction and fell into deep unrecoverable or irreversible confusion. "And the LORD came down to see the city and the tower, which the children of men builded. And the LORD said, Behold, the people is one, and they have all one language; and this they begin to do: and now nothing will be restrained from them, which they have imagined to do. Go to, let us go down, and there confound their language, that they may not understand one another's speech. So the LORD scattered them abroad from thence upon the face of all the earth: and they left off to build the city. Therefore is the name of it called Babel; because the LORD did there confound the language of all the earth: and from thence did the LORD scatter them abroad upon the face of all the earth" (Gen. 11:5-9).

That kind of unbelief led the descendents of Noah to fall further away from God. Fortunately, God still called out the person Abram from among the confusion of the time to establish a new generation to glorify His name among the people. God attempted to renew a covenant relationship with all humanity through Abraham and his descendents: "Now the LORD had said unto Abram, Get thee out of thy country, and from thy kindred, and from thy father's house, unto a land that I will shew thee: And I will make of thee a great nation, and I will bless thee, and make thy name great; and thou shalt be a blessing" (Gen. 12:1, 2).

After the death of Abraham and Isaac, the children of Jacob hated dreams and prophecy and sold their own brother Joseph who was the dreamer and messenger to God's covenant with Abraham. They got rid of Joseph, and the land fell into a drought and was barren just like their lives. All God wanted to do was to be with His people, but He was continually denied.

The drought of the land and the lack of food was the result of the disobedience of the children of Jacob. When Joseph's brothers sold him, they were rejecting God's very presence and His message. But God blessed Joseph in the land of Egypt, and eventually Jacob's sons repented from their wickedness.

Whether one is faithful or thousands are faithful, God is still present there. For His name's sake, God didn't forsake the children of Israel but remembered the covenant made to Abraham, and He raised up Moses to deliver Israel from the bondage of Egypt and bring them back to Canaan. After freeing the Israelites, God not only guided them by speaking through Moses but He gave instructions for them to build a physical structure for Him to dwell in. So they built the sanctuary in the midst of their camp according to God's commands (Exod. 25:8, 9; 29:36-43).

Unfortunately, God's covenant with the Israelites didn't last long before they succumbed to wickedness and the pursuit of their own desires. God raised up prophets to communicate and strengthen the sanctuary ministry. But the children of Israel rejected the prophets and their messages and killed most of them, leaving themselves in the hand of their enemies. In the land of captivity, many of them cried bitterly because they could not help themselves. Their undefeatable defense was always God—God was their dependable Captain and General.

Finally, God came to dwell among humanity, intermingling Himself with His creation (Matt. 1:18; Luke 1:35; Heb. 2:14-17; Gal. 4:4). The incarnation took place as the blessed hope of humanity. All of God's efforts to obtain a closer connection with humanity ended in death. Christ was crucified on the cross as if He was the one who was cursed. God's saving purpose toward humanity was, is, and will be immutable. In spite of the fact that humanity killed Christ, God established another covenant with His people through the earthly/human sanctuary ministry; thus, converted believers became the sanctuary of God (1 Cor. 3:16; 6:19, 20; Eph. 1:22, 23; 2:18-22; Gal. 2:20; Eph. 3:19; Col. 2:9, 10).

Through His Word God said, "For through him we both have access by one Spirit unto the Father. Now therefore ye are no more strangers and foreigners, but fellowcitizens with the saints, and of the household of God; And are built upon the foundation of the apostles and prophets, Jesus Christ himself being the chief corner stone; In whom all the building fitly framed together groweth unto an holy temple in the Lord: In whom ye also are builded together for an habitation of God through the Spirit" (Eph. 2:18-22).

At the time of Christ's death, the veil in the temple was torn from top to bottom, signifying that the priestly ministry on earth was finished. The blood of Christ had once and for all settled the payment for the sins of the world. "For there is one God, and one mediator between God and men, the man Christ Jesus; Who gave himself a ransom for all, to be testified in due time" (2 Tim. 2:5, 6).

With this kind of radical change to the system of the sanctuary ministry and the cessation of animal sacrifices, Jesus ordained a new covenant relationship with His children as their High Priest. That is the reason He is the Lord our righteousness and the Desire of Ages.

Even with His unceasing love, Christians have failed God. Rather than be the temple of God, many believers have shifted to antinomianism or legalism. This shift has weakened the working power of God in Christendom. The war between legalism and antinomianism among Christians is often the source of the division of denominations and the world's religions. This is putting God to shame and crucifying Christ afresh daily. In one way or another all of us are victims of antinomianism or legalism.

The following list is a cause-and-effect analysis that demonstrates how the good news of God's grace has been hindered by His people throughout the ages. However, the sanctuary truth is, fortunately, more dominant than the negative forces that try to stop God's message of love.

- Adam and Eve – sinned and disobeyed God
- Noah's children – built the Tower of Babel, a self-redeeming act
- Abraham's descendents – sold Joseph and rejected God's messengers
- Moses and the children of Israel – turned away from God to legalism
- Prophets – the people disregarded their messages
- Jesus – the people crucified Him and rejected God in the very act of killing His Son
- Christian era – fell into antinomianism

- Adventist message – many struggle with legalism and fear of lack of understanding in the message of the sanctuary ministry

Conclusion of the Matter

The solution for the problem is very simple. We must come to Christ as we are without covering up our false self-righteousness. Covered up righteousness is the worst of all types of open sin. Covered up righteousness is hypocrisy, which Christ warned against.

The solution for all human problems and sin is to approach the cross, repent of our sins, and go and sin no more. Christ calls us and says:

"Come unto me, all ye that labour and are heavy laden, and I will give you rest. Take my yoke upon you, and learn of me; for I am meek and lowly in heart: and ye shall find rest unto your souls. For my yoke is easy, and my burden is light" (Matt. 11:28-30).

"Ho, every one that thirsteth, come ye to the waters, and he that hath no money; come ye, buy, and eat; yea, come, buy wine and milk without money and without price. Wherefore do ye spend money for that which is not bread? and your labour for that which satisfieth not? hearken diligently unto me, and eat ye that which is good, and let your soul delight itself in fatness. Incline your ear, and come unto me: hear, and your soul shall live; and I will make an everlasting covenant with you, even the sure mercies of David" (Isa. 55:1-3).

Certainly, Christ is our righteousness for those who humble themselves and come unto Him, seeking a true sanctuary relationship with Jesus, the Father, and the Holy Ghost and asking God to dwell in you. That is the utter call of Jesus in Matthew 11:28-30 and Father and Holy Ghost in Isaiah 55:1-3. Read again the wonderful messages of Scripture that clearly define the perfect covenant relationship we can have with Christ as we become the sanctuary of God (1 Cor. 3:16; 6:19, 20; Eph. 2:21, 22; 3:19).

By following the Holy Ghost no one will ever be mislead: "Howbeit when he, the Spirit of truth, is come, he will guide you into all truth: for he shall not speak of himself; but whatsoever he shall hear, that shall he speak: and he will shew you things to come. He shall glorify me: for he shall receive of mine, and shall shew it unto you. All things that the Father hath are mine: therefore said I, that he shall take of mine, and shall shew it unto you" (John 16:13-15).

The solution for the aborted relationship of God and believers with God and with one another is fixed by Christ's self-sacrificing love and the Father's everlasting covenant and the Holy Spirit's everlasting comfort and guidance to all the truth. Now, there is no excuse for anyone to be lost or not receive atonement from God. This is the sanctuary ministry, the abiding in unity with our Creator and one another.

When Christ dwells in us, we can spread the gospel of Jesus Christ to all humanity with power from the Holy Ghost and true manifestation or vindication of the character and nature of God. "And after these things I saw another angel come down from heaven, having great power; and the earth was lightened with his glory" (Rev. 18:1).

This message in Revelation 18 is irresistible, incomparable, and irreversible. It will be spoken by men and women who have directly received the call and heard the true voice of God from the heavenly sanctuary just before the close of probation. The message will be irresistible because it will be spoken clearly and profoundly, warning the world of the last cup of the wrath of God.

The prophet Joel foresaw the preaching of this important message. "And it shall come to pass afterward, that I will pour out my spirit upon all flesh; and your sons and your daughters shall prophesy, your old men shall dream dreams, your young men shall see visions: And also upon the servants and upon the handmaids in those days will I pour out my spirit. And I will shew wonders in the heavens and in the earth, blood, and fire, and pillars of smoke" (Joel 2:28-30).

This message, empowered by God, will be delivered by Christians who accept the true message of the deliverance of Christ Jesus and who are willing to share the last message of the warning of God with the world. No one will escape the final wrath of God. But those who embrace the message of God's love will weather the trials because God is dwelling in them and giving them power and strength.

The entire earth will be enlightened because the Light of this world is involved directly. No discrimination of sex, gender, status, age, etc., will take place. God is calling everyone to be involved: "I will pour my spirit upon all flesh," sons and daughters, old women and men, professionals and servants.

Everyone who believes in Christ's redemptive work of atonement, no matter their background, will deliver the message to all kindred, nations, people, and tongues with the power of the blood of Christ and fire of the Holy Ghost and the very presence of God the Father. This is the evidence of enlightenment of the true gospel of Christ and the illumination of the entire earth.

The gospel of the sanctuary is the ministry of reconciliation. Those who accept it are commissioned to get involved in the ministry of spreading the gospel as Christ directed to prepare all creation for the coming of Christ (Matt. 28:18-20; Rom. 8:19-23; 2 Cor. 5:18-20).

The urgency of the commission is more imminent than ever before. The same voice of Jesus that spoke face to face with the disciples still echoes today in our ears.

> "And Jesus came and spake unto them, saying, All power is given unto me in heaven and in earth. Go ye therefore, and teach all nations, baptizing them in the name of the Father, and of the Son, and of the Holy Ghost: Teaching them to observe all things whatsoever I have commanded you: and, lo, I am with you always, even unto the end of the world. Amen" (Matt. 28:18-20).

> "And all things are of God, who hath reconciled us to himself by Jesus Christ, and hath given to us the ministry of reconciliation; To wit, that God was in Christ, reconciling the world unto himself, not imputing their trespasses unto them; and hath committed unto us the word of reconciliation. Now then we are ambassadors for Christ, as though God did beseech you by us: we pray you in Christ's stead, be ye reconciled to God" (2 Cor. 5:18-20).

Christ, our High Priest, beseeches us today to urge our fellow human beings to be reconciled with God. The call is not from anywhere else, but from the very Advocator of all humankind in the heavenly sanctuary at the throne of God. We must spread the word before billions of people end up in the graveyard without a saving knowledge of the Redeemer of the world because of our negligence. A time is coming when our faith will be tested and pushed to its limits, and we must be ready. No earthly technology or science or increased knowledge will save us when the world comes to a close.

> "And I beheld when he had opened the sixth seal, and, lo, there was a great earthquake; and the sun became black as sackcloth of hair, and the moon became as blood; And the stars of heaven fell unto the earth, even as a fig tree casteth her untimely figs, when she is shaken of a mighty wind. And the heaven departed as a scroll when it is rolled together; and every mountain and island were moved out of their places. And the kings of the earth, and the great men, and the rich men, and the chief captains, and the mighty men, and every bondman, and every free man, hid themselves in the dens and in the rocks of the mountains; And said to the mountains and rocks, Fall on us, and hide us from the face of him that sitteth on the throne, and from the wrath of the Lamb: For the great day of his wrath is come; and who shall be able to stand?" (Rev. 6:12-17).

> "But the day of the Lord will come as a thief in the night; in the which the heavens shall pass away with a great noise, and the elements shall melt with fervent heat, the earth also and the works that are therein shall be burned up. Seeing then that all these things shall be dissolved, what manner of persons ought ye to be in all holy conversation and godliness, Looking for and hasting unto the coming of the day of God, wherein the heavens being on fire shall be dissolved, and the elements shall melt with fervent heat? Nevertheless we, according to his promise, look for new heavens and a new earth, wherein dwelleth righteousness" (2 Pet. 3:10-13).

The great intellectuals, leaders of nations, captains in the military, scientists, mathematicians, engineers, historians, theologians, and philosophers will not be able to save themselves. Human intelligence is not a refuge or protection from the plagues that are soon to come upon the world. It is the responsibility of those who are called by God to bring the message of hope and the redemption of Jesus Christ to all people through the power of the Holy Spirit. "For I am not ashamed of the gospel of Christ: for it is the power of God unto salvation to every one that believeth; to the Jew first, and also to the Greek" (Rom. 1:16).

The very existence of the sanctuary message, which is taking place in the heavenly sanctuary, is for the purpose of awakening us to bring hope to the hopeless in this world. Very soon Christ will close the door of the sanctuary and the ministry of reconciliation and atonement will be complete and Jesus will come again. Then the old dragon, Satan, will be arrested and imprisoned in the bottomless pit for 1,000 years while the redeemed of God will investigate all the works of God to determine if God was fair and just in all His judgment.

"And I saw an angel come down from heaven, having the key of the bottomless pit and a great chain in his hand. And he laid hold on the dragon, that old serpent, which is the Devil, and Satan, and bound him a thousand years, And cast him into the bottomless pit, and shut him up, and set a seal upon him, that he should deceive the nations no more, till the thousand years should be fulfilled: and after that he must be loosed a little season. And I saw thrones, and they sat upon them, and judgment was given unto them: and I saw the souls of them that were beheaded for the witness of Jesus, and for the word of God, and which had not worshipped the beast, neither his image, neither had received his mark upon their foreheads, or in their hands; and they lived and reigned with Christ a thousand years. But the rest of the dead lived not again until the thousand years were finished. This is the first resurrection. Blessed and holy is he that hath part in the first resurrection: on such the second death hath no power, but they shall be priests of God and of Christ, and shall reign with him a thousand years" (Rev. 20:1-6).

After the thousand years reign of the saints with Jesus Christ, Satan will be released, and he will attempt to mobilize all the nations from four corners of the earth to fight against Christ and the saints in the New Jerusalem.

"And when the thousand years are expired, Satan shall be loosed out of his prison, And shall go out to deceive the nations which are in the four quarters of the earth, Gog, and Magog, to gather them together to battle: the number of whom is as the sand of the sea. And they went up on the breadth of the earth, and compassed the camp of the saints about, and the beloved city: and fire came down from God out of heaven, and devoured them. And the devil that deceived them was cast into the lake of fire and brimstone, where the beast and the false prophet are, and shall be tormented day and night for ever and ever" (Rev. 20:7-10).

Satan will fail. The victory will go to the Lamb of God who was slain for the redeemed. This old earth and heaven will disappear, and death and hell will be cast into the lake of fire, and all those not found in the book of life will be cast into the lake of fire, too.

"And I saw a great white throne, and him that sat on it, from whose face the earth and the heaven fled away; and there was found no place for them.... And death and hell were cast into the lake of fire. This is the second death. And whosoever was not found written in the book of life was cast into the lake of fire" (Rev. 20:11-15).

Now, all the interruptions of the covenant relationship of the sanctuary of God and humanity will be completely over. The complete reconciliation or atonement will be recreated between God and His people. All darkness will be removed, and the new morning will dawn for the redeemed.

"And I saw a new heaven and a new earth: for the first heaven and the first earth were passed away; and there was no more sea. And I John saw the holy city, new Jerusalem, coming down from God out of heaven, prepared as a bride adorned for her husband. And I heard a great voice out of heaven saying, Behold, the tabernacle of God is with men, and he will dwell with them, and they shall be his people, and God himself shall be with them, and be their God. And God shall wipe away all tears from their eyes; and there shall be no more death, neither sorrow, nor crying, neither shall there be any more pain: for the former things are passed away. And he that sat upon the throne said, Behold, I make all things new. And he said unto me, Write: for these words are true and faithful. And he said unto me, It is done. I am Alpha and Omega, the beginning and the end. I will give unto him that is athirst of the fountain of the water of life freely. He that overcometh shall inherit all things; and I will be his God, and he shall be my son" (Rev. 21:1-7).

Once and for all the eternal unity of God and His people will be restored to what it was like before the fall. Instead of dwelling among His people in a wooden sanctuary, God will be with us. Instead of dwelling in His people through the Holy Spirit, God will be with us. We will now be able to commune with Him face to face. As a living sanctuary, God will literally dwell with His people as John the Revelator revealed in the closing book of the Bible.

> "And I heard a great voice out of heaven saying, Behold, the tabernacle of God is with men, and he will dwell with them, and they shall be his people, and God himself shall be with them, and be their God" (Rev. 21:3).

> "And I saw no temple therein: for the Lord God Almighty and the Lamb are the temple of it" (Rev. 21:22).

The structural temple or sanctuary will not be needed after the second coming of Christ because Satan and sin will have been eradicated from the world and death will never be a threat in the new heaven and new earth. No reconciliation or atonement ministry will be needed because there will be no more sin. God and His people are once and for all united. God the Father, the Holy Spirit, and the Son will be the sanctuary.

The Creator and Redeemer of the world will restore His creation and once again enjoy everlasting unity with them. But we must be ready! Are you?

Abortion of the Sanctuary Truth

1) Adam & Eve ⟹ Sin

2) Noah's Children ⟹ Built Tower of Babel as Self-Redeeming Act

3) Children of Abraham (Jacob) ⟹ Sold Joseph & Rejected God

4) Moses (Children of Israel) ⟹ Turned away from God to Legalism

5) Prophets ⟹ Tribal Rivalry

6) Jesus ⟹ Crucifiction... Rejection of God by Killing His Son

7) Christian Era ⟹ Antinominism

8) Adventist Message ⟹ Legalism & Challenges of Fear or Lack of Understanding in the Message of Sanctuary Ministry

Fig.4

We invite you to view the complete
selection of titles we publish at:

www.TEACHServices.com

Scan with your mobile
device to go directly
to our website.

Please write or email us your praises, reactions, or
thoughts about this or any other book we publish at:

TEACH Services, Inc.
P U B L I S H I N G
www.TEACHServices.com

P.O. Box 954
Ringgold, GA 30736

info@TEACHServices.com

TEACH Services, Inc., titles may be purchased in bulk for
educational, business, fund-raising, or sales promotional use.
For information, please e-mail:

BulkSales@TEACHServices.com

Finally, if you are interested in seeing
your own book in print, please contact us at

publishing@TEACHServices.com

We would be happy to review your manuscript for free.

www.ingramcontent.com/pod-product-compliance
Lightning Source LLC
Chambersburg PA
CBHW060546100426
42742CB00013B/2474